Hamlet II
Prince of Jutland

Macbeth Speaks

An English Education

three plays

by

John Cargill Thompson

diehard
Edinburgh

diehard
publishers
3 Spittal Street
Edinburgh
EH3 9DY

ISBN 0 946230 34 X
Copyright John Cargill Thompson 1995

British Library Cataloguing in Publication Data
A catalog record for this book is
available from the British Library

The publisher acknowleges the financial assistance of the Scottish
Arts Council in the publication of this volume.

Other **diehard** drama

Klytemnestra's Bairns, Bill Dunlop
Hare and Burke, Owen Dudley Edwards
Gang Doun wi a Sang, a play about William Soutar,
by Joy Hendry
Port and Lemon, the mystery behind Sherlock Holmes/*Laird
of Samoa*, John Cargill Thompson
Cheap and Tearful/Feel Good, John Cargill Thompson
*What Shakespeare Missed/Romeo & Juliet: Happily Never
After/The Marvellous Boy/Cock-a-doodle-do!* by John
Cargill Thompson.
A Matter of Conviction/Parting Shot/When the Rain Stops,
by John Cargill Thompson
The Lord Chamberlain's Sleepless Nights, a collection of
plays by John Cargill Thompson

currently at the printers

Alcestis, by George Buchanan
Cutpurse, by Bill Dunlop

To
Sarah

Hamlet II: Prince of Jutland

First presented at Sheffield Crucible
  8th March 1984
  Hamlet – Oliver Beamish
  Directed by John Ashby
This version reproduced for 1995 Edinburgh Fringe Festival
  at Café Royal, venue sponsored by Caledonian Breweries
  Rik Forrest as Hamlet.
  Directed by Adam Sunderland.
(Evening News Special Capital Award 1993).

Macbeth Speaks

First presented at the Harry Younger Hall, Edinburgh
  12 August 1991
  Macbeth – Seamus Gubbins
  Directed by Iain McAleese.

An English Education

First presented at Mull Little Theatre
  22 April 1993
  James I – Robin Thomson
  Directed by Eric Bennett.
(1994 Scotsman Fringe First Winner).

Characters in the Play

Cargill Thompson   Shakespeare

Hamlet: Prince of Jutland . . . .   **Hamlet**: Prince of Denmark
Feng: King of Jutland . . . . . .   **Claudius**: King of Denmark
Horvendile: his brother . . . . . . **Old Hamlet**
Geruta: Queen of Jutland . . . . . **Gertrude**: Queen of Denmark
Corambis of Elling, ... **Polonius**
   a Councillor
Hilda: his daughter . . . . **Ophelia**
Her **six brothers** . . . . **Lærtes**
Olaf & Haakon, two bluff jarls .   **Rosencrantz & Guildenstern**
Rorek Slyngebond, King of   or vice versa
   Denmark, father to Geruta & Wigleck
Wigleck, Prince of Denmark,
   Hamlet's uncle
Alsi: King of Lindsay (Lincoln),
   blood brother to Feng & Wigleck
Orwenna: his ward, Queen of
   East Anglia, Hamlet's wife
Hermuthruda: an almost virgin
   queen of the Picts, Hamlet's
   girlfriend
Ruth and **Mabel** have no place in
   the story
Jarls, Courtmen, Huscarles, the
   Palace cook, a **shot-putter**,
   and of course
Yorick; an out-of-work actor . . **Yorick**
   resting as a wine waiter

Hamlet II
Prince of Jutland

This production is promenade in the sense that Hamlet is able to dispense with set and talk directly to the audience. He must, however, consider the positioning of the few props required by the action: the Skull, books (including a paperback copy of Shakespeare's play), box of sharpened wooden stakes and sword.

Hamlet enters and appears to count the audience

Hamlet: We're a select group aren't we ... the seekers after truth ... ah well, it is not something everybody can take, is it? Truth can be very disconcerting ... sometimes one doesn't want to believe in anything ever again ... Well, do you remember when you discovered what it was they were actually doing? ... Quite a shock wasn't it? ... My mummy and daddy don't do that, no?

Sings

> What is truth and what is fable,
> Was it Ruth or was it Mabel?
> Does it matter what is said,
> When a man is gone and dead?

Not bad that, is it, for a chap who used to dodge bard classes to go fishing!

Sings

> I am dead and gone, lady.
> I am dead and gone!
> At my head a grass-green turf,
> At my feet a stone!

Well, which do you like the best? ... That was Shakespeare my great biographer ... That's the lad I'm competing with ... The same tune, different words ...

Sings

> A pickaxe and a spade, a spade,
> And a bloody great winding sheet,

> And a pit of clay that has been made,
> For such a guest to greet!

Ay, that's both of us mixed together ... which is probably what we'll end up with ... Go to Bard School, Go Directly to Bard School, Do Not Go Fishing, Do Not Go To The Pub, and Do Not Collect Two Hundred Kisses from Ruth, Mabel or anyone else until you have learnt how to tell your own story clearly and succinctly in your own words ... Otherwise before you know where you are, some punter will have done it for you, and you'll be terribly confused about who you are ... That's me ... Terribly confused about who I am ... I must come somewhere between that Jesus Josephson chappie and Adolf Schikelgruber in the "Who's Had Most Written About Them" stakes, and yet the more I read the more confused I get.

Indeed I am beginning to think that may be the whole idea ... They encourage you to get confused at higher and higher levels till they make you a doctor of philosophy or something and let you set about the confusion of others ... What have we got here? "What Happens In Hamlet" ... You know I wouldn't have thought it possible to keep so bloody close to the story and yet transform it altogether so wonderfully as this play does ... A little light on laughs, perhaps, and he hasn't quite recaptured what a bloody twit I was ... but it's a good read, well worth £2.95 of anybody's money ... and that's the trouble, isn't it? ... When your ambitious bard starts in biographing people long dead ... He becomes obsessed with giving his public a good read at the expense of little inconveniences like truth or who actually won ... I lost ... I allowed that grinning little pot-bellied windbag Wigleck to catch me with an understrength army before the battle season was properly open ... And so I become Hamlet's ghost and fodder for crows and ballad-mongers ... and now you lot are probably as confused as we were when Wigleck's huscarles suddenly started coming at us out of the mist ... and I can assure you that it is very, very confusing to have half a hundred sweaty vikings erupt in front of you, waving their battle-axes and screaming a fighting chant at the top of their voices:

Sings

> Follow, follow, follow
> We will follow Wigleck,

> Anywhere, everywhere,
> We will follow Wigleck!
> If we go to England we will overcome.
> And when we are in Jutland
> We will make them run! ... run! ... run!

Why do battle chants have to be such appalling poetry? ... Maybe it has something to do with the fact that poetry requires a modicum of thought while kicking people's heads in doesn't! ... But who is this Wigleck I hear you ask? ... For in spite of the hundreds of millions of words ... words ... words written, chanted ... shrieked and ranted about me, Hamlet ... he ... the actual winner is not a name that rings any bells ... Come on, own up ... Anybody here ever heard of Wigleck? ... Sometimes, by those who've had the benefit of a real classical education at a school your government hasn't got to yet, called Wiglerus? ... Exactly!

Sings

> He is quite forgot-ton, lady
> He is quite forgot-ton!

He was my uncle ... Ha, ha ah! ... You are a set of smug clever-clogs aren't you? ... We've all heard of Hamlet's uncle, haven't we? ... You thought he was called Claudius, but if I say he was called Wigleck I probably know best ... after all he was my uncle and you can hardly blame Shakespeare for changing a name like that ... Wigleck! ... I suppose it's alright for a clown with a red nose and white make-up all over his face, but it's a no-no in tragedy, isn't it? ... Don't underestimate names ... They're very important ... They tell us who we are ... If you are called Romeo you can go round saying things you'd probably be locked up for if your name was Albert or Harold ... How many Janes do you know who act like Esmereldas? ... It's like if I'd been called Trevor ... He wouldn't have had a play would he? ... "This is I, Trev the Jute, I prithee take thy fingers from my throat" ... or ... " 'Tis sweet and commendable in thy nature, Trevor" ... Those Elizabethan punters wouldn't have stood for rubbish like that ... The peanuts and popcorn would have been flying stagewards before the end of the first scene *(acts as if dodging missiles)* "Hey leave over ... Give us a break ... WE didn't write the bloody stuff ... It's that William Shakespeare!" ... but you are all on the wrong track ... Shakespeare did not change Wigleck's name ... He left him out ...

Wigleck was an uncle ... but not that uncle ... He wasn't *(consults the copy of the play)* Gertrude's ... second husband ... Her real name by the way was Geruta and she was the daughter of Rorek Slyngebond, King of the Danes ... Hey that's a good one, isn't it? Rorek Slyngebond ... It has similar connotations to your 'Sly Boots' ... Wigleck was his son, Geruta's brother and a prince of Denmark ... Which I wasn't by the way ... None of you pick up on "Trev the Jute!" ... You did! ... Yes I am a Jute ... Calling me a Dane is like asking a Scot what's the largest "lake" in England? ... Then telling him it's Loch Lomond ...

You've got "Trivial Pursuit" as well have you? ... Don't trust the answers! ... Claudius was actually called Feng, which I'm sure we are all agreed is an excellent name for a dog and he wasn't, as you shall discover ... but I didn't ... Well not until it was far too late ... He wasn't my uncle at all ... Now do you see why you'd better go to those bard classes? ... This is not as easy as I thought it was going to be, is it? ... I thought all I'd have to do was sing a few songs to warm you up ... tell my story clearly and succinctly and then off back to Valhalla before the All-Father noticed I'd been away ... Well he's only got one eye ... forget it ... load of heathen ... I've begun at the wrong place, haven't I? ... I think I need a drink and then we'll start again ... You lot just talk among yourselves till I get my act together.

He appears to consult between books and papers while humming and drinking from his skull

... Yes, it is a real one, madam ... you needn't look so shocked ... I didn't kill him or anything ... I inherited it, in lieu of a bad debt ... It belonged to some actor chappie called ... Yorick! ... Alas, poor Yorick ... a fellow of infinite jest, of most excellent fancy ... Where be your jibes now? Your gambols, your songs, your flashes of merriment that were wont to set the table on a roar? ... Not one now to mock your own grinning! ... And he's got something to grin about, hasn't he? ... Two bottles of wine a day? ... Give an actor that and he's your friend for life.

Takes another drink

Now you understand the origin of the phrase "pissed out of his skull", eh! *(offers the audience a drink)* ... And you'll not take a drink with me? ... alright! So what have you heard then? ... That

I'm some kind of death figure par-excellance with a horror of coloured neck-ties ... a manic would-be suicide wandering in and out of other people's bedrooms, stabbing elderly politicians in the arras? ... Only in slightly more formal and poetic language! ... Sorry to disappoint you but it is quite impossible to sum up my story in tight little academic aphorisms like "Poison, play and duel" ... It is a sprawling and immensely complicated tale:

Sings

> Hamlet Horvendilson Favoured of Odin
> Subject since cradle days
> To strange strokes of fate.
> Bow sings, steel bites
> Shafts fly from strong arms,
> Red runs Hovendile's sword,
> Ravished is Svafa;
> Ere homeward the dragon ships
> Carry Geruta.

(Breaks off and mutters to himself) or should I begin with my other Grandfather Gervendile Cutthroats? ... You see this is the way we told our stories ... with a lot of name dropping, right back to Odin if possible ... so, before my tale can even get to me you learn how my father Horvendile had, after defeating and ravishing Svafa, own sister to Coll, King of Norway, on the quarter-deck of her own ship, had as a reward, been given in marriage Geruta, daughter of his overlord Rorek King of the Danes ... then you get a succession of potted and not so potted puffs on everybody in the family, until you've either forgotten, or which is worse, don't care anymore, whose story it is in the first place, ... Well it's mine ... the chap in the black frock with the skull who you've been given to understand is always on about being and not being ... It is the story of I, Hamlet, who wasn't Prince of Denmark ... and that's what you are going to get ... and perhaps a little more than you bargained for ... because you see it is twice as long as you thought it was with lots of fascinating revelations about things you don't know ... like the bit about Hermuthruda, an almost-virgin Queen of the Picts ... Shakespeare probably heaved her because to be consistent he'd have had to call her Hermentrude and you just cannot have someone called Hermentrude in a tragic drama ... It's even more absurd than Wigleck. *(refers to play)* Who

else is gone? ... *(mutters)* Alsi, Orwenna ... Hil ... no, she's here ... Ophelia, mmhm! *(speaks to audience again)* It is not a bad job, is it? ... Some marvellous stuff ... I don't know what it all means, but good stuff ... and you see he wasn't there ... I was ... He has missed the joke ... The delicious irony of the games the gods play.

You see I am or should be ... and maybe will be when you've heard the story from my own lips ... one of the great "He might have been" boys ... like your Georgie Best and the Right Honourable David Owen ... and this play ... "Hamlet Prince of Denmark" ... in spite of all its splendid poetry is a lie, before which, Hamlet Prince of Jutland is banished to a few dusty footnotes at the back of the more expensive editions ... This one doesn't even mention me in the introduction, but then what do you expect for £2.95? ... There is a whole section about a possible pre-Shakespearean version and whether this lost masterpiece is by Kyd, Marlow or even Shakespeare himself ... but Hamlet the man is quite overlooked ... just Stratford make-believe, along with Anne Hathaway's mulberry tree and Shakespeare's drinking exploits.

And so once again where do I start? With Horvendile's ravishment of Svafa? ... A deed talked about for weeks afterwards in our part of the world ... It had four poems written about it! ... *(refers to his Shakespeare again)* How does this play start? *(mutters)* Old Hamlet murdered by Claudius ... Claudius marries Gertrude ... "My father's spirit in arms! all is not well; I doubt some foul play" mmhm *(raises his voice again)* How about the slaying of Horvendile, whom you've probably gathered by now is Shakespeare's Old Hamlet by his brother and joint King of Jutland ... Feng ... in the bedroom of Horvendile's lovely lady wife, my mother, Geruta? ... Fratricide and incest already ... and unless you studied Macbeth your year, you know roughly where we are ... "In the rank sweat of an ensemened bed, honeying and making love over the nasty sty!" ... Come off it me loves, brothers don't kill brothers in their wives' bedrooms without good reason ... He'd caught them at it ... a wonder it hadn't happened years before ... Feng and Geruta had been feeling guilty and each other almost since the day they'd met ... "We really shouldn't dear!" ... "It'll just complicate things ... but isn't it good!"

The affair was managed with the utmost discretion and everybody took care not to bother Horvendile with a lot of mischievous court gossip ... "It isn't as if he's losing anything by it ... I'm sure he's much better off with that Brunhilda who doesn't seem to mind if he comes to bed a little bibaceous" ... It was such an unlucky chance, wasn't it? that made him stumble into the wrong bedroom when Feng and Geruta were ... what's that nice phrase of Shakespeare's? ... making a beast with two backs!

You know Horvendile didn't even recognise them at first ... He was apologising and leaving them to it, when Geruta said "Oh blow!" ... or something like that, and sat up suddenly and he realised he'd better do some marriage guidance ... Just picture it, our two overweight gutlings instinctively leaping out of bed on opposite sides ... covers all over the place ... comical! but it saved their lives ... if they'd stayed where they were Horvendile would have got them ... as it is he is quite unable to resist screaming at his wife ... "whore, strumpet, drab, bitch, jade, trol" ... eurgh! ... He really shouldn't have turned his back on Feng, should he ... not with the walls hung with battle-axes ... All this guff here ... about it being given out that Old Hamlet had been stung by a serpent while sleeping in his orchard actually was our official communique, as released for bards, soothsayers and other disseminators of court gossip ... like all Official Communiques you are not meant to believe it ... and nobody did ... The fiendish cleverness of Official Communiques lies in the "Back Up Story For Those In the Know" ... who by pronouncing of some doubtful phrase as "Well, well, we know" or "We could", and "if we would", and such ambiguous givings out will soon put it about that Horvendile in a drunken fury has attacked the King of Denmark's daughter in her own bedroom and if it hadn't been for good old Feng she'd be dead and we'd be at war with her father ... Pity about Horvendile, chap said he drank too much!

It's brilliant, isn't it? ... Damn it, it's the truth! ... a few things left out ... the context altered ... but essentially the truth ... That's the way to tell a lie, isn't it? ... resist the urge to embroider ... "Where've you been?" ... "At the office, dear!" ... Of course you were at the office, but your secretary was there too! ... the art of good falsehood is to tell the truth, not the whole truth, but if you can manage it, nothing but the truth ... if the story sounds right nobody asks the awkward questions ... like what was Feng doing in my mother's bedroom in the first place ... after all everybody knows he spends a lot of time there. It's fine for everybody else ... there is peace in Jutland ... Feng marries Geruta ... after a decent period of court mourning of course ... but I have a blood feud on my hands ... eight years old, that's all I am and I'm saddled with a bloody blood feud.

I liked Feng, I'd always liked Feng ... I liked him a damned sight better than I'd ever liked Horvendile ... and this is my first Revelation ... It was not revealed to me ... at this point ... what I am about to tell you I won't find out till much later on ... but as everybody else knows it and as it does help you to appreciate the delicious irony of things I will reveal to you now ... *(whispers)* ... Feng ... is ... my ... father! That changes things doesn't it? ... Why the hell don't people tell things to eight year olds? ... Feng had killed the man I'd been brought up to believe was my father and so by the rules that even an-eight-year-old knows, I was honour bound to kill him ... That was our way, when somebody was killed it was the duty of their nearest blood relation to avenge them ... the blood feud ... and so not knowing any better I set about being petulant and convincing myself that I hated Feng and my mother for marrying him ... He becomes my bogey-man and I get him terribly confused with an outbreak of vampirism I'd heard somebody talking about ... Do you know what my great plan for killing him was? I was going to creep up upon him when he was asleep and drive a stake through his heart! ... I used to go around collecting little bits of wood and sharpening them ... I had a box under my bed full of the things ... If they'd just told me the truth I could have had a normal childhood, taking the dogs for a walk, burning the odd village, marrying the daughter of the king of the marsh next door and so on and so forth ... as it is because no-one has told me whose son I actually am, I have to screw myself up to make more and more serious threats against a very nice chap.

You can't expect an eight year old to work this kind of thing out for himself ... It's obvious when you know ... that's why he hadn't drugged my bedtime drink, shoved me in a sack and tipped me over the nearest cliff ... but it hadn't occurred to you till I told you. It didn't even occur to Shakespeare. The trouble was he kept smiling at me! ... "Oh villain, villain, smiling damned villain, that one may smile and smile and be a villain!" ... I was very confused, but by the time Feng got round to appreciating just how confused I was, it was too late ... He'd put off the little parental heart to heart just a little too long ... You cannot call a seventeen -year-old youth who is planning to drive a stake through your heart into your back room, offer him a drink and tell him you're his father ... not if he's a complex youth who'd just love an excuse like that which would let him off the hook ... that might have worked if I had indeed been the child of dull old Horvendile ... but the son of Feng had the intelligence of Feng and therefore he was just as big a fool.

Didn't I promise you farce not tragedy? Feng knew that in my place he'd take the drink, pretend to accept the story and then by and by when all suspicions were lulled ... Tchoo *(gesture of throat cutting)* ... and so very regretfully ... but for the good of Jutland ... I'm not being cynical, haven't I made it clear that he was a good king who put his subjects before himself? Well if I haven't ... he was ... and so for the good of Jutland he decides I will have to be terminated ... I knew at once ... the smile wasn't in his eyes any more *(pause)* Help! Help! Help! Up to this time it has been a game ... I cut little pointed sticks and one day I'm going to stick one in Feng ... the fantasy of a disturbed seventeen-year-old ... now suddenly, there is an imminent outbreak of poisonous snakes in the grass *(consults his Shakespeare)* What does it say here? ... But come:

> Here, as before, never, so help you mercy,
> How strange or odd soe'er I bear myself,
> As I perchance hereafter will think meet
> To ... put ... an ... antic ... disposition ... on!!

In other words that I am going to act mad ... It has caused a lot of confusion that madness hasn't it? ... There are whole treatises about how mad I am ... Very! ... But in craft ... nor' by nor'west as the saying goes ... I can tell a hawk from a hernshaw.

Vikings, as I have hinted so long as they abide by the rules of the blood feud can kill almost anybody ... "almost" ... there are exceptions; a society that doesn't have exceptions becomes far too cut and dried and you miss the delicious torment of seeking "The Way Out" ... Our exceptions were "The Favoured of the Æsir"

... a little euphemism for the mad ... You were strictly forbidden, however many blood feuds you had in hand to kill those whom the Gods favoured ... again it all fits into place when you know the facts ... this makes all that rabbiting on about camels and fishmongers ever so much clearer doesn't it ... it makes the treatises on Hamlet's madness a bit redundant ... but once you appreciate that as long as I keep up the pretence of being only half a shilling I'm safe, everything is clear ... The ball is now in Feng's court ... He's got to prove I'm twelve pence, and until he does I can go around saying all sorts of things and generally stirring it up ... I had a "whale" of a time ... everybody began remembering my curious behaviour as a child ... Feng of course wasn't fooled for a moment but he has got to prove beyond reasonable doubt to everybody that I am not mad before he can do a thing.

Now, there was in Jutland, at this time, one of those elderly politicians who have outlived the people's hate ... you know, the sort of fellow whose reminiscences of the raids of fifty years ago are invested with a wry humour that implies that things have been going to the dogs ever since ... and this man ... Corambis was his name ... Corambis of Elling ... Corambis had a daughter called Hilda ... You know them as Polonius and Ophelia ... ooh! that Hilda! ... Fair skinned and full of promise ... as half the court, the male half, were prepared to acknowledge ... alright madam, I grant there were some questions about her chastity, but you don't need chastity when you look like Hilda!

(sings)   Come away, come, sweet love!
           The golden morning breaks;
           All the earth, all the air
           Of love and pleasure speaks!
           Touch our arms then in embrace,
           Join our wet lips in a kiss,
           Mixing souls in mutual bliss;
           There's no folly or disgrace
           In flying, dying in desire
           Burning, turning in your fire *(stops suddenly)*

Ssh! ... There's somebody behind that bush ... Oh, ho! I see it ... clever! ... a trap to establish my sanity; well I am not so easily caught ... "Are you honest? ... Are you fair? ... Get thee to a nunnery ... Why wouldst thou be a breeder of sinners? ... To a nunnery, Go!" ... Turning up a dish like Hilda in a lonely wood is incontestable proof of lunacy ... or something weird ... Lucky for me her father stood on a hedgehog.

The tale he carried back of my rejection of his daughter really set the cat among the pigeons ... Geruta was distraught ... a little genteel madness she was prepared to overlook ... after all it can happen in the best families ... take Jack the Ripper ... but the implication that I might not be interested in the little ladies touched her to the core ... after all everybody says it's the mother's fault, don't they?

I was summoned! ... "My Lord, the queen would speak with you ... and presently!" *(make sure the old meaning of 'presently' equalling 'at once' is brought out)* Is this another test ... Is mummy against me now? ... I dare not take the risk ... and so I give an exhibition of gratuitous madness that would have won first prize at a psychiatric conference ... I hop about flapping my arms like a cock ... bark like a dog ... and prowl round the room clawing at the wall hangings ... miaow! miaow! miaow! ... oh, there's method! ... This way I get to look under the bed ... and what do I find? ... as well as that! ... a rat! a rat! at first I thought it was the rat and that the blood feud was over ... Hopefully I turn the body on to its back ... "Thou wretched, rash, intruding fool, farewell! I took thee for thy better: take thy fortune; thou findst to be too busy is some danger!" ... Yes, it was just poor old Corambis of Elling and I have another blood feud on my hands ... not this time with a slightly balding veteran who's shy of open violence ... but with Hilda's six brothers who've been itching for an excuse to get at me ever since I insulted their little poppet in the woods ... Yes, Laertes times six! ... and that is far too many, even for someone my size ... and don't forget I am Feng's son and intelligent enough to appreciate that sometimes the wisest thing to do is scarper ... You see the old insanity plea doesn't get me out of this one ... It doesn't work this way round ... Being a loony protected you from being killed but it did not give you carte blanche to go round killing other people as and when you felt like it ... Anyway it was the six Corambis sons who were mad ... though not in a "touched by the Æsir" way, if you follow my drift.

I did manage to buy myself a little extra time by chopping the old man's body into little pieces and stuffing it down the palace privies ... not very subtle, eh? ... but Geruta was having hysterics in her bedroom and the corridors were full of punters trying to find out what it was I'd actually done ... Even so I nearly got away with it because of course you cannot start a blood feud till the body's been found ... Unfortunately, a couple of days later the fair Hilda, curious about what she'd just been doing, is startled to discover her father, or at least his head, staring up at what someone his age definitely should not have been staring up at ... and certainly not his daughter's ... Take my advice, if you ever need to dispose of a body, don't shove the head down the loo ... it causes a blockage ... and a head is all you need to start a blood feud!

I had just three days' grace to get out of the country then the boys would be after me ... Feng was terribly helpful ... England would be best ... we'd lots of relations there, and the locals were all a bit touched by the Æsir so I'd blend in quite nicely ... he gave me a firm man to man handshake, money, and a letter to an old comrade of his called Alsi, King of Lindsay - that's Lincoln and around there - you know what was in that letter don't you? ... You don't ... One of the Macbeth people, I suppose ... Instructions to kill me instantly on arrival ... no, it is not nearly as bad as it seems here *(refers to play)* This is where our way of telling stories, where you give c.v.'s of all the main characters, has something to recommend it ... Feng, Alsi and that Wigleck chap, who hasn't come into the story yet, had in their youth gone through a ceremony of blood-brotherhood ... you know, my quarrel is your quarrel and that kind of thing ... So it's not nearly as cold-blooded as Shakespeare makes it ... in fact it is quite a compliment really ... Feng admires me enough to fear me as a rival ... and of course he is protecting me from the sin of parricide which never goes down well with the Æsir and can complicate one's entry to Valhalla ... He's safe enough because, as you know, crimes undertaken, if you are a King or something like that for the good of the state, aren't on your personal tally at the final reckoning ... and so with two bluff jarls, who don't know what they're letting themselves in for ... to look after me and see the letter is delivered ... Haakon and Olaf ... the pair you know as Rosencrantz and Guildenstern ... and equally disposable ... we set sail in the most splendid little boat:

Sings

> Fringed round with goldwork,
> Builded of strong black oak,
> Valiant the vessel
> To bear the young prince.
> Under her dragon sails
> Face turned to farthest shore
> Journey he must the blood feud to break.

Again I've got to explain the rules haven't I ... if I can stay hidden for three years Corambis' sons can't touch me ... That boat should have tipped me off, shouldn't it? ... I should have guessed it was a father's gift to speed me to the supernal pleasures of Valhalla ... Anyone arriving there with a boat like that and two stout jarls at his back will be assured of his place in the front line of Odin's shieldwall when the Last Battle starts ... I just thought it was a conscience present, and that was really stupid of me because being a King Feng doesn't have a conscience ... I really appreciated it because a little trip to England was just what I needed to think things out ... maybe I should just take to the Swan's Bath and become a hero *(explains the phrase Swan's Bath for the audience:)* ... go on a viking cruise or two! ... still I wanted to keep my options open ... I hid my little box of stakes, you remember the ones I'd carved when I thought Feng was a vampire ... they were important to me, a symbol of lost childhood ... and I gave my mother new tapestries for the banqueting hall as a going-away present and ... this is just the kind of over-dramatic thing seventeen year olds go in for isn't it? ... I made everybody swear that if I hadn't returned for my 21st birthday party my death should be presumed and a great memorial feast held in my honour ... the birthday baked meats could coldly furnish forth a funeral feast ... Then my mother gave me my father's royal ring and I was on my way ... Do you remember what I said about the Æsir playing little games with us? ... This bloody ring was exactly what I needed ... a duplicate of the one Feng had used to seal his letter to Alsi ... with this in my possession I am obviously going to open that letter, aren't I? ... and I did ... and I discovered his little arrangements ... and I change the names so that it is Haakon and Olaf who will be killed. Thus "Rosencrantz and Guildenstern go to" and I become Alsi's palace cook's porter.

You don't know this bit, do you? ... This is new stuff ... yes, he left it out. I don't blame him, it's complicated ... so pay attention - this wasn't on your A-level course ... *(staccato one-liners)* We land; I fade into the crowd ... The Jarls are killed; everything goes back to normal except that I've got to eat. The options are: steal, beg, or get a job as a soldier. I try begging which includes casual portering for the palace and being a big fellow I see off the opposition and become the regular porter ... clear so far? ... I call myself Curan, which means in the Welsh "The Wonder" and keep out of everybody's way ... That is, until the coming of Alsi's ward Orwenna, who will become the Queen of the East Angles when she marries; until that time Alsi is looking after her kingdom ... She wants a husband ... Alsi likes things just the way they are ... East Anglia's good for a sizable chunk of income tax and it doesn't cost him all that much in Unemployment Benefit.

What have the political differences between Lindsay and East Anglia got to do with the saga of Hamlet the Jute? ... Alsi it seems had promised Orwenna's papa that the girl should be married to the goodliest man in the kingdom ... That's a nice open-ended one, isn't it? ... there can be plenty of debate and off-putting with something as vague as that ... but even the English can't argue all the time and in the breaks there were sports.

One thing that has always puzzled me about the English is their obsession with games ... the way they get into such ludicrous frenzies over people kicking sheep's bladders around with the people who support one group beating hell out of the followers of another in such a possessive way ... Anyway on this occasion they were throwing things ... not for once at each other ... just throwing them as far away as they could ... I started to laugh ... It was very funny, a load of brawny huscarles grunting and sweating under the weight of huge stones they could hardly get off the ground ... But of course the one thing you must never, never do at an English sporting contest is laugh ... You can scream all the abuse you like, urinate on your fellow spectators, kick people's heads in, but you must never, ever laugh ... Everything stopped ... Everyone was looking at me ... "Could I do any better?" ... "Great Pillock!" ... The next thing I know I'm in the centre of the ring trying to lift the stone ... It's heavier than it looks, but I get it up ... knee height ... waist height ... then with a great heave on to my shoulder ... and I hurl it from me at least four paces beyond the longest throw.

Way ho! ... They'd been about to lynch me, now I'm a hero ... somebody tells him I'm his Welsh porter and he insists on being introduced to me ... Well, I give him the salute of Feng's courtmen but luckily he doesn't recognise it ... and asks if I'm married? I laugh and say something about being too poor to maintain a wife, and he laughs too and gives me a bag of gold ... "Now that I have the dowry how would I like a bride?" ... I think it's some sort of royal joke and go along with him, I mean you do if you're talking to kings ... but he's seen his chance ... Who's the goodliest man in the kingdom? I am ... at stone-throwing. All he has to do is make a lot about this being a sign from the Æsir and force the marriage through. The East Anglians are not going to accept the palace cook's porter as King ... so he gets to keep East Anglia. When I jib a bit, he starts babbling about cosy little dungeons where a lad could have a good long stretch and lots of peace and quiet to think things over, so I decide that it is probably best just to go along with things ... maybe it is just another royal joke, eh! ... only it isn't! ... and Orwenna is hurriedly thrust into a wedding dress ... Now is brought forth the golden loving cup ... and a soldier ... actually the lad who had thrown his stone closest to mine, which was very English and sporting of him, don't you think? ... and my master, the palace cook, step forth to back a comrade and witness a wedding.

You get the picture? ... "It is our custom," says the grinning Alsi, "That the bridegroom should display his bride price" ... and at this point he's expecting me to produce that bag of gold I'd just been presented with ... but I don't ... I produce this little darling! *(displays Royal Ring)* Yes, Horvendile's ring ... a King's ring ... The Royal Seal of Jutland ... and that wipes the smile off his face ... pronto! ... within minutes everybody has worked out just who I am and a great shout of laughter shakes the hall ... Poor Alsi ... he has to pretend he knew all the time ... and he gets away with it! ... It's just the kind of dramatic wooing the English go for in a big way ... I'm surprised Shakespeare didn't use it ... except he's got to cut something and if he'd brought in a wife in Act Four he'd have added another hour at least ... Eh! but what a scene! ... The rafters ring with cheers ... My mates from the kitchen bring out more wine ... everybody's drinking horns and embracing each other ... Skoal to Hamlet Horvendilson ... Skoal to Orwenna, Hamlet's wife ... Skoal to the King and Queen of Jutland and East Anglia!

And this changes things quite a lot doesn't it? ... Feng thinks I am dead ... well even in our day secret letters between rulers were risky things couched in the obliquest language ... Alsi wouldn't have risked sending a detailed description of the execution of Olaf and Haakon but simply said "Your commands have been carried out!" or something to that effect, and as it wouldn't have occurred to Feng that I'd have this ring and play silly buggers with his Royal Warrant, he'd take that to mean that I was dead and tell his bards to put it about that I hadn't survived the voyage or English cooking or something like that, and as it had been my last request, the funeral would not be celebrated until the date of my twenty-first birthday. More madness, but a dead madman could be safely humoured.

The proof that something like this had happened was that nobody had looked for me and I had had two and a half years peace and tranquillity - but as you all know a Royal Wedding really shakes up the bardic tonsils ... and mine was a godsend ... I'd spent two years ogling her from afar as a vegetable porter ... Well that's the line they are all going to take! ... "That for love of her I had put off the royal state" ... They love that sort of thing ... hit song material ... The Princess and the Swineherd ... if I don't get to Feng's hall before the songs you can bet your shirt I will be bitten by a serpent while sleeping in my orchard ... at least according to the Official Communiques.

No dilly-dallying now ... Action ... There are not quite two weeks till that funeral–birthday party of mine back in Jutland ... If I leave immediately I can be there before songs or letters ... But it must be immediately ... And so with everybody's good wishes ringing in our ears, Orwenna and I, oh so romantically disappear ... and of course everybody nods and winks ... honeymoon couples, particularly royals, often disappear ... "a little cruise, eh?" ... but far from lazing on the royal yacht we are in fact hot-footing it back to Jutland in one of those drab little fishing boats that work out of Grimsby.

We have pulled it off ... I'm home with three days to prepare for the dramatic re-appearance ... The night before my funeral I slip secretly into the palace and repossess myself of this little box of sharpened kindling sticks ... remember them? ... The symbols of the childhood I never had! ... I note the new hangings in the banqueting hall and the preparations for tomorrow's feast ... To be fair to Feng he's done me proud ... There are to be whole roasted oxen, swans ... at least twenty different kinds of seafood ... and hundreds and hundreds of loaves of bread ... There are even vegetables for the peasants ... Hey! this wine's good ... Rhenish? no, Alsatian ... most moreish! ... but I must refrain; I'll need a clear head and a firm hand tomorrow.

At noon I return, having torn my clothes in the obligatory lunatic manner, and covered myself in cow-dung ... Picture it! ... The hall is dark, light streaming in through the great open door ... The torches as yet unlit ... a tall figure ... me ... stands framed against the light of day ... For two strides I am no more than an outline ... God? ... Man? ... A Ghost? ... many are already half-lost in drink and the silence is everything I can wish for. In three years a boy of seventeen comes to his full strength. I must look to some, especially those who agree with me as to the quality of the wine, as a man would who has spent those three years drinking with the Æsir ... then someone laughs and I am their old friend mad Hamlet once again. Feng has half risen from his seat with a look so piteous in purport, part yearning, part appeal, a father's look, eh? ... but that doesn't occur to me ... and he recovers quickly and his greeting is warm enough ... and now everybody is laughing and calling for more drink. Someone asks what it is I've got under my cloak? Does Feng recognise this little box think you? ... remember these sticks? ... The symbols of the childhood I never had? ... If he does he doesn't show it! ... He is the model of a modern monarch at ease in his own hall ... but the questions continue ... "Where's old Haakon and Olaf?" ... "Hey, is it true about English girls, eh?" ... "Are you still mad?"

If Feng's performance is masterly mine is better ... Since entering the hall I have not uttered a single word, just smiled and nodded as if I am quite overcome by the splendour of the assembly ...now I speak for the first time, hesitantly, as if not quite sure where I am or how I've got here ... "Good friends ... Great King ...

for so I take it you must be ... I think you mistake me for someone
else ... I know not of Haakon and Olaf or indeed of any Jarls ...
and it is not fitting I speak of the wantonness of English girls
here ... " and I look at my mother ... who lowers her eyes and
blushes ... "I am a simple man, Curan is my name, Curan of
Grimsby, for the last three years a porter in the service of Alsi
King of the Jutes of Lindsay, but now a wanderer in search of
songs and stories ... Hearing that you kept wassail here, and that
there was a tale to be told I come in hope of earning my night's
lodging as your singer and cupbearer" ... and at that I snatch a
harp from one of the skalds and begin the first stanza of the
"Drappa of Grettir the Strong":

Sings

Bold was the hero to enter the hall
Where the sound of the gleewood bade welcome to all:
"The Wassail bowls brimful, your door stands ajar
Will you turn from your benches the hero from far?
I come with strange stories and wonders to tell,
Having travelled to Mikkelgard, Littern and Hell;
Are you prouder than Odin to thus say me nay,
Will you be the first to turn me away?"

As I sing I keep my eyes locked upon those of Feng, for the
story of Grettir the Strong is the story of a man with a father's
killing to avenge and I wanted him to know that his time was
come.

I had not fooled him for a moment, oh perhaps when I'd first
entered he had shared the doubt as to whether I was indeed Hamlet
... three years had changed me ... but he knows his own son ... He
know that it is Miching Mallecho and that I mean mischief ... It's
my move again; I've set up this marvelously dramatic entry and
he just does nothing ... now I am wearing a sword and I've got my
little box ... what the hell do I do? ... Just finish "Grettir the
Strong"? The longer I go on singing the more I lose the effect of
that entry ... I draw my sword ... that gets everyone on their feet
... "I will fight for the right to join your company" ... This is
more like it, isn't it? This is confirmation that I need a straight
jacket ... so they humour me ... "Have a drink, old chap" ... "Let
me take this!"

Oh, Feng you are marvellous ... the croaking raven doth bellow for revenge but you're not to be frightened by false fire, are you? A lesser man would turn me away with a crust, you laugh with the others at the rare jest of a man playing the butler at his own funeral feast ... and you've got my sword ... "just put a couple of nails through this lest he should do himself an injury and the blame be ours" ... oh yes it is safely fixed into its scabbard by the time it's returned to me. I can't hurt myself with it and I can't hurt anyone else.

Who's that he's speaking to? ... Don't you recognise them ... The six sons of Corambis ... Yes that is a key ... He is giving them the key to the chamber in which I shall be tonight ... That is clever, your blood feud can be served tonight, there is no need for any unnecessary disturbance of the Law and Order of Jutland ... "Let him have his feast, after all it is his funerals that we celebrate!" ... oh, they're laughing now ... "Skoal to the memory of Hamlet Prince of Jutland" ... and I smile and pour for them and Feng leaves his place ... He will go to his room ... I have counted on this ... it is his custom.

Do you see this? *(He shows the audience a phial of powder)* Yes, with this in their wine the rest will sleep ... see it works upon them already ... and to my plan which has been three years a-hatching! ... Quickly I slashed at the top of the wall-hangings ... Do you understand now? I pull them over the sprawling revellers and take those stakes and hammer them down ... Don't they look sweet, my pretty babes ... You know what they are for now! ... The hot blood of Jutland is caught like a shoal of herring in my net ... Feng can scream as much as he likes, you'll be a while getting out of that.

Damn it, the man's asleep ... You know I have come for a reckoning yet you sleep ... *(mimes trying to draw sword)* ... They've nailed it fast ... It is not for me to question what the Gods give ... and I exchange my nailed-up sword for his ... "Wake, King! ...'Tis I, Hamlet the Jute! ... Sir, though I am not splenetive and rash, yet have I in me something dangerous! Which let thy wiseness fear!" He laughs ... I scream at him that this is the end of power, of applause, of comfort, sweet murmurings ... and of incest ... and still he laughs as he tries to draw my sword and now I'm laughing as he falls entangled in the coverlet.

Hysterically I strike and strike and strike and he is dead, dead, dead ... and still I fear him ... Then Geruta my mother is pulling at my shoulder ... "What have you done?" ... What a stupid question! ... Feng's body lies mangled on the floor an arm's length from his head ... Surely it is obvious what I have done! ... "I have avenged my father ... I have avenged Horvendile your husband" ... "Oh Hamlet thou has cleft my heart in twain" "Then throw away the worser part of it and live the purer with the other half ... assume a virtue if you have it not" ... She is wiping the blood from the head and making as if to rejoin it to its trunk ... "Looby, here lies your father!" She starts to laugh uncontrollably. "Slain by his own get!" ... "No! No! No! I loved my father, forty thousand lovers could not with all their quantity of love make up my sum!" ... "You really are mad! Can't you see, it was not a real father that you loved but the idea of a father ... the terrible masculine honour of the blood feud" ... and she is down on her knees imploring ... "Oh ye Gods, teach this boy love before it is too late ... if it must take the blood of every living thing cherished by him ... teach him to love that he may at the last understand the love I felt for this man ... This I ask in the name of Frigga and of Baldur ... this I ask as weregeld for the blood of Feng" ... I could feel the Æsir hear this terrible oath ... and I knew now without doubt that her words were true.

It explains so much doesn't it? Why he hadn't had me killed, why he had smiled so bloody much. The Gods have such a rare sense of humour ... The enginer was hoist with his own petard ... and now there were two of us upon the floor trying to stick the head back on to that lifeless body ... I had killed my own father and he was going to freeze in Hell because that damned sword that would not draw lay beyond the reach of his clutching fingers. He had died like a beast in his bedclothes without even a weapon to give him comfort.

Then I remembered all those jarls tucked up in the hall tapestries ... They shall speak for Feng in the hall of the Æsir ... I who was mad in craft was at that moment mad indeed ... He shall have honour and company on the road to Valhalla ... I shrug my mother from my arm and snatching a torch from the wall return to the feast ... everything was as I had left it an age ago ... Courtmen and Jarls sleeping under their wraps, arms linked in drunken comradeship ... "Well comrades you have failed your king! When Feng needed you where were you? ... Gunnar where you? ... And you Einar that swore always to guard his back? ... Well Feng needs you now ... He needs your escort to the Gods" ... and I light the pyre ... none escape:

Sings

> Humbled the proud jarls burning in Jutland
> Fierce flame from smoking thatch shoots high,
> In that day dire danger fails not.
> Guard him to Gladshein hall of the Gods
> Housing for hero slain by his son.
>
> He shall sit with the Æsir
> Till the last horn is blown!
> He must sit with the Æsir
> That was slain by his own!

Refers to his Shakespeare again

Well obviously he couldn't just end it like that ... too vulgar! ... almost Hollywood isn't it? ... You can't burn a theatre down for every performance ... But it's close ... The same and not the same ... I do return and people do get killed ... but not me ... not me! ...We haven't got to Hermuthruda yet! ... I didn't believe it ... that I who had been so scurvily treated would just fade away like a bubble in the air in an irrelevant little fencing match with an amalgam of Hilda's six brothers ... I thought at first some punter was going to dash on at the last minute and say I'd recovered ... and everybody ... including Fortinbras, who'd be the son of that Svafa Old Horvendile ravished on the quarter-deck of her own ship would grovel as I sweep on for the grand walk down in fish-net tights and a brand new frock and invite everybody to come and see Part Two next week ... I mean if Henry IV and Henry VI can have a second part surely I deserve one? ... I'm twice as successful as they are! ... but no that was it ... finito!

> "Let four captains
> Bear Hamlet like a soldier to the stage,
> For he was likely, had he been put on
> To have proved most royal."

Of course he was quite right ... I blew it didn't I? Bubbles time! ... And he was far too good a bard to let me ... I'm so tempted to stop here, with the crown of Jutland on my head ... a hero in his hall ... well friends, scratch a hero and you find a fool! ... You have to be a fool to be a hero ... sensible people get themselves a nice number and raise kids and barley ... heroes push their luck!

Remember Wigleck? ... Remember Orwenna? ... Remember Hermuthruda? ... I wish I didn't! ... I may be King of Jutland but just think of the mess killing all those stout jarls and courtmen has left! ... Oh I made the conventional military coup speech of course ... you know, the one with all the lies and rhetoric about taking vengeance on behalf of the people against the wicked forces of greed, privilege and oppression ... and they cheered me in the way the mob always cheer winners ... and then my troubles began!

It is all very well having experience as a kitchen help ... indeed I would recommend it to all would-be rulers that at some point in their training they do their own washing up and clean a few boots ... If your Alfred had done a little of that kind of thing he'd never have burnt those cakes ... but it's not enough ... It may make you popular, but leaders need to be more than popular ... they need to be able to lead, to accept responsibility, to resist being popular! ... me! ... I love it! ... I'm the great white hope ... young, tall, and all essential equipment in fine working order ... and I've been so lucky I think I've got the Gods on my side. Well, look at it, I've got everything ... a pretty wife ... two kingdoms ... the people's love ... and this is the point where Shakespeare draws the line, has me killed off and the rest is silence! ... in fact my uncle Wigleck succeeds old Rorek as King of the Danes and Alsi siezes Orwenna's little kingdom of East Anglia.

Two problemettes for the hero ... which does he tackle first? ... Oh I was convinced I couldn't be defeated! ... I mean kingdoms had been dropping into my lap ever since I'd taken up shot-putting! ... I fancied taking on Wigleck ... but Orwenna wanted to go home ... We went to east Anglia ... and do you know it was all a terrible mistake ... Alsi hadn't annexed it at all ... Whatever put a silly idea like that into my head? ... He's just been looking after it for us, what with all those evil buggers in Wessex and elsewhere casting the beadies on it ... Isn't that kind! ... and we get drunk together ... Well I get drunk and he remains together!

Has anybody got anything to stop this bloody headache? ... God, my mouth's like the floor of a troll's cave! ... eh? I haven't? ... I have ... I have agreed to do the cunning old swine a little favour ... I have promised to go to Edinburgh on his behalf and ask the Lady Hermuthruda, Queen of the Picts, if she'd like to marry him ... the name meant nothing to me then either ... One didn't really talk about Picts in polite circles ... *(whispers)* Peculiar courtship rituals ... that kind of thing. To put it bluntly if you wanted rumpo you had to beat her with a battle-axe.

You see his ploy now ... He was Feng's blood-brother remember! ... sworn to kill me or at least contrive my death ... He may not be a hero and have plays written about him but he is not bad at the little schemes ... and this is one of his best ... He can't lose ... either he gets Pictland - South East Scotland to you - not a bad consolation prize considering the Edinburgh tourist industry! ... or ... what he's really after ... my immediate translation to Valhalla, via Hermuthruda's battle-axe.

In blissful ignorance of all this I arrive in Edinburgh ... at first I think I'm having problems with the accent - "You'll hae to fecht ... Jimmy!" ... could mean anything ... then remember "My luck" ... I have developed a real hero's capacity for ignoring all the bad things and believing I can't lose ... So that when Hermuthruda is terribly sympathetique I don't see the catch:

Sings

> Who prostrate lies at women's feet
> And calls them darlings dear and sweet;
> Protesting love and craving grace,
> And praising oft a bonny face:
> Are oftentimes deceived at last,
> Then catch at nothing, hold it fast.

You see if I'd only gone to those bloody bard classes I used to plunck, I would have known that nine times out of ten your tragic hero is betrayed by the "other woman" ... but I had gone fishing instead, I'd been kissing Ruth and Mabel, ... remember? ... So when Hermuthruda offers to overlook the "fechting" and suggests we attack Alsi instead ... I put it all down to my good luck, and having all essential equipment in fine working order.

Oh, I could dress this up ... distort the truth a little, a war of righteous indignation ... Revenge, revenge, Hamlet revenge! ... Don't be so naive ... I'm an erection dragging a bird brain in its wake ... I am utterly besotted by a pair of long pictish legs ... you can forget the righteous war theory ... there is no such thing ... That is a fantasy of the masculine ego ... I learnt that fighting alongside Hermuthruda, ... that women have an innate good taste which stops them from trimming the butcher's apron with the spangles of chivalry. They massacre children, burn good farmland ... and ... poison ... their ... rivals.

Yes, Hermuthruda "liberated" Orwenna ... You see why Shakespeare stopped when he did? ... That's my tragic hero status, buggered! ... Take away his black clothes ... Do not have any soliloquies! ... Do not go to Valhalla! Jealous wives have their place in a tragic tale ... It would have been quite alright for Orwenna to see off Hermuthruda ... that would have been community chest cards towards being a hero ... but see the other way round! ... You're zapped ... out the game!

So that when Wigleck takes up his bit of blood feud upon my return to Jutland ... everybody deserts ... even my darling Hermuthruda sent him a little note on exotic stationary pointing out that the rule book, as it applied to almost-virgin Queens of the Picts, gave him certain entitlements to her body should he succeed in beating me.

I have just one final lesson to learn, haven't I? ... As I fling up my left arm to shield myself ... What left arm? ... My armour plates peel off with a wrench ... That's what that little hook at the back of a battle-axe is for, didn't you know? I seem to be looking up at those massed points of steel forever ... The rest should be silence, eh? ... It is so undignified to scream ... but I had to learn that final lesson ... The one Feng knew ... A man may live like a Hero and fight like a God ... but when he dies in battle he is butchered by as many as can get to his body ... so that everyone can have a heroic tale to tell of how they killed the tyrant:

Sings

> Does it matter what is said
> When a man is gone and dead?
> A pickaxe and a spade, a spade
> Not even a winding sheet,
> Just chucked in a pit that has been made
> For such a guest to greet.

Bow and Exit

Macbeth Speaks

Smoke effect. Eerie lighting.

Macbeth enters through the audience handing out pebbles to people.

(An English actor should not be alarmed by the 'Celticness' of the character. Macbeth is not a modern Scot, the language he would be speaking would be the Gaelic and the part is envisaged as Standard English with the occasional dialect word or turn of phrase to give colour.)

He wears a simple brown woollen robe, suggesting the hermit rather than the warrior.

Macbeth: Go on my dear, have a stone on me ... you? ... you? ... no!

Chuckles

   Isn't a bad reputation a terrible thing ... people won't share stones with you, eh?

Laughs

   Sorry! ... I can't help it, you all look so totally confused. Where do stones come into Macbeth, eh?

   That's the trouble they don't! Not according to William Shakespeare.

   Put 'em away ... but don't lose them ... they are a clue.

Blesses them in such a way as to provoke an ambiguous response.

   Bona dies et pax vobiscum.
   Why do you start and seem to fear things that do sound so fair?

Translates what he has just said.

   Good day and the peace of God be with you.
   God ... God ... God!

Yes, I have named my God and I am still here ... no red flash and a little yellow demon at my elbow to carry me back to hell.

And it's working, isn't it?
It is! You are confused.
Not your idea of Macbeth at all.
Pebbles and Paternosters.

But you see, that is just what it is about ... Stones and how to pray ... You can forget this anthology *(produces a copy of the play)* of bogeys and bewitchment ... The boy done well ... but it's not true ... Ay, the boy's done too bloody well hasn't he?

> "Macbeth was not a good man,
>   he had his little ways,
> And sometimes no one spoke to him
>   for days and days and days.
> At Christmas time the cards of cheer,
>   that stood upon his shelf,
> Were never from his near and dear,
>   but only from himself!"

Let's start with the facts:

> "The strong one was fair, brown haired and tall,
> Very pleasant was the handsome youth to me.
> Brimful of food was Scotland East and West,
> During the reign of the ruddy, the brave King."

That is contemporary ... well give or take fifty years ... It's about the only contemporary account that does survive ... I lost, remember, Shakespeare got that bit right ... and the winners write the record books ... But even creative history cannot ignore "Brimful of food was Scotland East and West" ... Twenty-three years of peace and prosperity ... Ay, it was really rather a dull time ... sorry! No murders, no magic, no kinky sex ... There was a little scandal about a shepherd in Sutherland ... but apart from that it was simple harmonious living ... "Brimful of food was Scotland East and West during the reign of the ruddy, the brave King." ... And I must be very careful here, mustn't I?

Macbeth has become a tradition ... Come on, disappoint a tradition and anything can happen ... oh yes, disappoint people in their expectations and what's left, eh?

Well what is left?
Fear and superstition.
This!
The play you know and love.

"When shall we three meet again?
  In thunder, lightning, or in rain?"

Frightened people can unloose a deal of uncontrolled energy
... oh ay, begin thinking scary and something scary will happen.

That is what happened.
To me.
It is, you know!
The rest of the world was thinking scared and poor old
Macbeth got caught in the ebb.

Throw this away, it's havers.

You know nothing ... not even the year I came to the throne
... Oh, don't worry about it ... I'd have been very surprised if any
of you knew that ... Not like 55 BC and 1066 ... your conquerors
wouldn't let you forget those, eh? ... no, forget those and you
might remember what it is to be free.

I came to the throne in 1034 AD.
Exactly!

One thousand years after the White Christ died on Golgotha to
redeem you all ... one thousand years after the most significant
event in Christian history ... the Passion of Our Lord Jesu Christ
... Believe me, there was some fear in the world then ...
everybody thinking "This ... is ... it! ... Second Coming Time ...
That is if He isn't here already" ... Stern vikings who've spent
half a lifetime in a veritable orgy of pillage, rape and arson,
falling over themselves to get to the few churches they've left
standing for a splash about in the Holy Water and a new name ...
You go up to some punter whom you've know from the cradle as
Thorkyll Bear Slayer, and he tells you he is now called Emmanuel
and doing voluntary work on behalf of the berserkers'
reformation society ... "Would I like to make a contribution?" ...
More altars collapse under the weight of all the swords and battle
axes being exchanged for strings of little brown rosary beads
than the last ten centuries have seen off in honest heathen havoc.

Don't worry about it ... There's no problem ... Employment for all, eh? ... Building bigger and better churches ... oh yes, the Church offers shelter ... well, to Christendom ... everybody else is scared shitless, but Christendom is sheltered.

So what's gone wrong?
Hadrian's bloody wall.
Confused again?

Because of Hadrian's wall we Scots are not sure if we are in Christendom or not ... you see we'd joined before you lot when all the rules and regulations hadn't been fully negotiated ... and we weren't paying the same dues as everyone else ... our monks ... we call them culdees ... walk in the footsteps of Podraig and Callum ... Patrick and Columba to you ... not Peter and Paul.

Yes ... that makes us more vulnerable than our friends the Odin worshippers, eh? ... they at least have beastly habits to give up and be amnestied for.

We Celts ... ooh! ... we are doing really naughty things aren't we?
Celebrating Easter on a different day.
No Treasures.

Our priests getting married and having children instead of getting a bit on the side from their housekeeper.

Fine! ... Even this sort of depravity can be overlooked provided your attitude to Church property is sound.

The Celtic Church didn't have any property.

Come on, a Christian Church without possessions, a church that gives rather than takes, it's not on, is it?

Still got those stones I gave you? ... pass them round ... you were beginning to wonder when they were going to come in, weren't you?

We did have buildings ... but they were functional ... For our great festivals we prefer to gather in the old tribal places.

Exactly! ... The stone circles of our ancestors.

We haven't a clue about their original purpose ... why should that bother us for God's sake? ... Our Christianity isn't jealous of anything that has gone on before it ... They are our heritage, we know there cannot be anything bad about that.

What is an altar? ... Just a slab of stone, eh? ... The same stuff you are passing round only bigger ... No, we are not superstitious about stones, superstition comes with guilt ... we just appreciate the comfort they can give.

Come on, who hasn't picked up pebbles on the sea shore, eh? ... and then spent one of those marvellous silly evenings sorting and re-sorting them ... ay, and if you've a sister quarrelling over the best ones ... not bad quarrels, fun quarrels, with cuddles for making up ... we've all got a stone somewhere in the house ... one that we can't bring ourselves to throw out, eh? ... It's been there since you were a child.

Yes, I had one ... a great big family stone ... called Lia Fail ... The Stone of Destiny ... It was big enough to sit on.

Ay, when I sat on Lia Fail, I was conscious not only of rubbing arses with all my predecessors, but that I was in direct contact with the bones of Mother Scotland.

And they lost it ... They lost the Lia Fail.
How can anyone lose a stone that big?

Very easily if you've forgotten what it means ... if it isn't a family stone anymore ... just one that has been left behind by the punters who where living here before you.

God, I'm getting gloomy ... Come on, let's have some more light on all this and to hell with bogeys and bewitchment ... you shouldn't make love in the dark.

As lights come up he reacts in mock surprise.

Oh yes, I try to keep up ... of course I do, I am a civilised being ... I have an enquiring mind ... but it is very difficult to fully appreciate the wonders of a culture that is not your own ... I mean, one always thinks one has got it right, doesn't one?

Pointing to the lights

To me that is just a smidgen suspicious ... Light for the

asking ... command our night and day ... I don't understand it ... it must be witchcraft ... or extreme sanctity ... Oh yes, in my time you either got burnt or made a saint if you could do things like that ... There was a laddie ... but to hell with him, you can all do it now, can't you? ... just by pushing a piece of plastic ...

Looks closely at the audience

No! ... You are not all saints, are you? ... you certainly aren't, I know that smile ... don't waste it on me, I'm a married man.

Yes ... man.

Take my hand if you don't believe me ... go on, take it ... Well, tell them ... my flesh doesn't burn with the fires of hell, does it? ... Possibly it's a bit sweaty ... that's natural ... I'm scared of you ... Face of Christ, I'd rather stand in the shield linden waiting for your bloody ancestors to erupt out of the mist than be here on my own trying to tell you about something that not only doesn't exist any more, but has been replaced by one of the greatest plays ever written ...

> "Tomorrow, and tomorrow, and tomorrow,
> Creeps in this petty pace from day to day
> To the last syllable of recorded time ... "

Marvellous!

It says here in the introduction that if Shakespeare hadn't written it I would be forgotten ... Here it is!

> "Just an obscure murdering little kinglet
> unremembered even in his own country"

> "Brimful of food was Scotland East and West,
> During the reign of the ruddy, the brave King."

I was Ard Righ n'h'Alba. High King of Scots.

And that's just words ... King? ... High King? ... so what?

I did not succeed because I was someone's son ... or because I killed someone's son ... I didn't oppress, rape or interfere with people's sheep ... I was elected to my place by people who had as much right to it as I had ... oh yes ... the Ard Righ was the elected guardian of a set of traditions that go right back to when we gave the Romans, poor bastards, such a hard time, they had to build a bloody great wall and order everybody to start pretending that the world ended there.

Oh yes, that's when it all started.
Your confusion.

The great Celtic Empire that comes down to you in charming little fantasies about Arthur, Morgan le Fey and the Lady Guinevere ... traded with Tyre and Zidon, with Egypt and Troy ... There was tin from this Island in Solomon's temple ... But the Romans told you we were a bunch of savages ... and Romans know best ... Well they are such decent chaps and they have given you a civilisation ... You owe them a lot ... all Europe does ... after all it's Rome that made the world possible for Christianity ... your kind of Christianity ... she created the framework ... Christendom was just an extension of Rome ... why do you think the Pope lives there ?

Have you got it yet?
The difference between my world and yours?

I'm so obviously inferior, eh? ... I've not had the benefit of a classical education ... oh yes, it took us Gaels and Celts that bit longer to find out all about those fascinating Roman gods and goddesses, you know, the ones with the exotic tastes in swans, bulls, and bondage ... ay, those ones, the ones that make sheep and welly boots seem normal.

Far from being a "petty murdering kinglet" ... I was High King of a confederation that stretched almost as far south as Greater Manchester ... and if any of you have ever been to Manchester you'll appreciate why we stopped there ... you can take the responsibility for civilising people so far and no further, eh?

Back to the introduction to the play, as if reading from it.

"An ambitious, self centred man seduced by evil visions and his wife's strength of will into killing his overlord ... finally destroyed by the very forces to which he has surrendered."

That is so Roman.
So bloody clear cut.

A conflict between good and evil ... with good very concerned about property and power ... ay, and possessions ... Don't you see, I didn't have any power ... at least not by some divine right ... I had responsibility ... of course I had possessions ... even Lenin had his own underpants ... but I wasn't obsessive about them ... How do I explain our sharings? ... You know how families can be very jealous of some things ... "Who's pockled the last cream cake, eh? ... That was mine!" ... but others are held in comfortable common? ... You see we hadn't had our natural generosity confused by conquest ... we didn't have one race of rulers and another of ruled ... oh yes, that's how important beating Rome had been for us ... we didn't have a class system ... we were all warriors and we were all peasants ... ay, even the Ard Righ ... I had to work in the fields just like everyone else.

It's a dream now, isn't it? ... perhaps it wasn't really like that at all ... because of course we did have our fair share of greedy hubristic bastards ... ay, like my cousin Duncan ... but we were certainly not, I assure you, a load of kilted barbarians running round going "Hooch!" all the time like those wallies that invade Wembley every two years.

So where does it come from? ... all this blood and witchcraft ... it's so very Scottish isn't it?

> "Warlocks and witches in the mirk,
> By Alloway's auld haunted kirk."

Come on, it's what you all think about whenever anybody mentions 'Macbeth' ... for God's sake, actors go absolutely bananas, clap their hands over their ears and start a frightful ritual that includes pulling each other's noses and turning round in circles with their eyes shut.

Consults play

I wouldn't mind if it was just me ... after all it does have a certain John Wayne ring to it:

> "Till he unseamed him from the nave to the chops
> And fixed his head upon our battlements."

But how can you do this to her? ... How can you do this to my Gruoch? ... You didn't even know she had a name did you? ... It was Gruoch ... it sounds like water gently stroking pebbles ... or the wind caressing heather ... It suited her.

Oh Gruoch, my lady ... granddaughter ... wife and mother of Kings.

How do you picture her?

> "..................... I have given suck, and know
> How tender 'tis to love the babe that milks me;
> I would while it was smiling in my face
> Have plucked my nipple from his boneless gums
> And dashed the brains out, had I so sworn as you
> Have done to this."

Oh, it's not Shakespeare's fault ... He didn't even understand the lie that is being told ... I should thank him, at least he's given it a kind of dignity.

You are right little man ... I was nothing without Gruoch ... and I am nothing with her.

Oh yes, I promise you the breath of her night robe bending a candle flame could make me sweat.

My dear, come here ... Face of God, you are so bloody beautiful ... hold me ... my mother, my daughter ... my love ... my friend.

Hey! ... shall I really confuse you now? ... mem?
Wait for it!
Lady Macbeth is Macduff.
No, I am not just being clever.

Don't you see? ... This story was first told for a far, far more sinister purpose than an afternoon's theatrical entertainment.

It was told to justify the destruction of a way of life.
It succeeded, didn't it?
Macduff was the King's name.
My name ... Gruoch's name.
For us the chief of clan Macduff had an almost spiritual authority.

Did you get it now? ... by inserting a fictional Macduff chief into the story as one of the leaders of the Junta that deposes me you gave it instant respectability.

Poor Shakespeare, he never really did understand why it was so important that I should be killed by Macduff and not Malcolm ... to him it was just a name in the chronicles.

"Beware Macduff!"

That is the Royal name. And the first of that ilk is my wife Gruoch.

Oh yes, Lady Macbeth is Macduff ... It is in her right and the right of her son Lulach that I have rule.

Ay, we came together at first in convenient friendship and respect.

Oh yes, when I began to realise I loved her I became scared stiff ... I could hardly touch her ... not easily ... love must be giving not taking.

And I am losing my credibility, aren't I? ... what happened between Gruoch and I is none of your business ... but this makes me so bloody angry ... Don't you see, it is what has been done to Gruoch that has torn me out of my grave to come here tonight.

You want a fiend-like queen? You want Shakespeare's Lady Macbeth? ... try the wife of my successor ... oh yes, Saint bloody Margaret ... she drove her husband to his death ... she stole common land to endow her church ... but she's a saint because she won.

Gruoch and I reigned peacefully for twenty-three years ... everybody had enough to eat ... Very unnatural ... we must have had some help ... a society without poverty and oppression? It must be witchcraft ... why, it undermines mother church ... The church thrives on poor people.

Read our old Celtic stories ... the ones that have survived Christian revision ... green ... green as the green hills of Erin ... full of strong light and colour ... no witches ... monsters, yes ... monsters to challenge a man's aspiration ... but the little darknesses of diablerie? ... no way I'm afraid.

About the only thing this punter's got right is my name ... Macbeth ... ay, and he even mispronounces it ... It is actually MacVaha ... It means son of life, from the same root as usque va ha ... water of life ... ay, whisky ... the connotations are equally ironic, eh?

I am MacVaha ... MacFinlay ... MacRuari ... MacCullen ... MacKenneth ... Macduff ... yes Macduff, Macduff, Macduff ... Macdonald ... MacConstantine ... MacKenneth ... MacAlpine.

That's roots.
That's where I come from.
Banquo!

A bit of a wimp part, isn't it? He's another invention ... doesn't come into the story for a couple of hundred years ... then suddenly, when the Stuarts need some ancestors, he turns up.

This is my problem, isn't it? There is so little relationship between historical truth and this play that it is almost impossible to relate the two.

You do appreciate this saintly King I'm supposed to kill ... Duncan ... wasn't ... wasn't a King ... well not of Scots ... he was under King of the Welsh of Cumbria.

Oh yes, it was Duncan that rebelled against me ... I am Duncan.

Confused again?
I think we'd better forget the play, eh? ... It's served its purpose, it got you here.

There is no mystery and no murder. Prince Duncan was killed in a rather scrappy sea battle by my kinsman Thorfinn Raven Feeder, Jarl of Orkney.

Ah ha! You don't know about Thorfinn, do you? Shakespeare had to leave him out or he'd have taken over the play ... he was Kirk Douglas and Tony Curtis rolled into one ... girls couldn't resist him ... a real viking ...

"Jarl Thorfinn stood by Odin's tree
A mighty axe in his hand held he. Out! Out!"

You see what I mean? As soon as I start talking about Finn I lose the thread.

Get back to Prince Duncan ... my cousin ... Grandfather's favourite nephew.

Oh yes, my grandfather ... the king ... wanted Duncan to succeed him ... that's why he got him elected King of Cumbria.

But it was I that was elected.
Duncan didn't like that.
My election made him very, very angry.
And so he invaded England.

That's surprised you, hasn't it? Come on, admit it, you were expecting me to say "Prince Duncan gathers together an army and marches northward". He wasn't a fool. That would have been rebellion.

Oh no, what he did was almost Byzantine in its complexity ... brilliant! You see only a de facto King can invade the territories of another de facto King. Private individuals just raid. Only Kings make war. The implication of Duncan's action is that Scotland is making war on England ... he says he's King of Scots and he's got eight thousand battle axes to back him up ... that's one way of getting your claim recognised ... It doesn't really matter that he is beaten and has to take to his ships ... It doesn't even matter that his eldest son Malcolm is captured ... in fact in a way it's all to the good ... the English have a different system to us ... as far as they are concerned Kings are succeeded by their eldest sons ... They honestly believe that they have captured the next King of Scots ... ay, and after Thorfinn's done the business they think they've got the King. There now follows twenty-three years of peace and prosperity ... Malcolm grows up ... in England ... what is it the Jesuits say? ... Give us a lad till he's seventeen and he's ours for life ... The boy is English ... give him his due he really does genuinely believe that because he's the son of a King he must be a King ... They take their titles so terribly seriously ... For twenty-three years he grows up ... they are very nice to him ... a good allowance ... dogs ... girls ... everything a healthy lad could desire ... and he grows more bitter every day ... you see there is one thing they won't give him ... an army ... They won't give him one, but they keep hinting that they might one day ... He's such a marvellous weapon.

So what happened?
I've told you.

Christendom was scared of us because we were different ...

Everywhere else, every square foot of land is accounted for ... our common ownership could give peasants ideas ... ay , and our church is far too free ... we actually talk about the meaning of God and the fallibility of his ministers ... we were definitely a threat ... you can't have different systems ... it undermines society.

The irony of it is ... that the end was almost an accident ... nobody actually made a dramatic decision to make war on the Celtic system. England had a problem ... Siward, Earl of Northumberland ... yes, the fellow in the play ... it doesn't do him justice ... he was another of these charismatic viking chappies ... like Thorfinn and that lad Thorkyll Bear Slayer I told you about ... The problem is he is refusing to trade in his battle axe ... he doesn't want a string of little brown rosary beads ... he wants to kill people ... I see your point, as far as you are concerned it is much better that he should kill Scots than other Englishmen ... so you lend him to Malcolm who is still asking for an army.

Twenty-three years of peace and prosperity up the spout because of an uncontrollable berserk.

We beat him.

Shakespeare's put two campaigns into one ... I told you to forget the play ... we beat Siward ... but the English have suddenly found a marvellous outlet for aggressive elements ... so when a punter called Tostig Godwinson ... a brother of that chap Harold that got beaten by William the conqueror ... becomes a little over aggressive and ends up raping a nun ... they lend him to Malcolm ... Can't lose can you? ... you either get your undesirable elements killed off for you or you conquer Scotland.

We weren't expecting them.
Not a second time.
Not so soon.

We are slow to muster ... we won so easily last year, time to get the crops in.

Where's Finn?

I don't believe it. Thorfinn Raven Feeder's got religion ... he's been born again ... Instead of standing on a raised shield firing up his huscarles he's on his knees playing with a string of little brown rosary beads.

All right, retreat.

The further we lure them into these mountains the easier the job will be.

And I make a fatal mistake.

Oh it's a sound enough strategy, stretch their line of communications to breaking point.

The only problem is I should have given orders to have the country they must pass through laid waste ... I should have left them nothing they can possibly make any use of ... not a bloody egg.

I can't do it ... I can't bring myself to ask people to destroy their children's food.

We'll still beat them ... its only a bloody raiding party for God's sake ... even God's against them, he's very possessive about nuns.

And we laugh and make our stand at Lumphanan in Mar.

See, I place the Boar's head here ... the men of Moray will form the shield ring ... you of Argyle stay our of it, I want you to harry their flanks ... but don't take any risks ... if we can't beat them tomorrow we simply retreat again ... it's a nuisance but I don't want any heroics ... we've got plenty of time ... this is our home ... whatever you may have heard, war is a sordid pastime ... its not a game of shinty ... Give me a hunk of that bread, I'm starving.

In the dim dawn twilight Scotland stands shoulder to shoulder ... of course we are afraid, damn it, we are imaginative civilised people ... but we know what we've got to do.

Then suddenly the bloody fog comes down.
I can't see a spear's length.
Is that you Dougal?
MacIan where are you?

Damn you, don't push, you'll have us all over! ... we are not advancing, but we are on the move ... I try to swing myself round

to see what is happening behind me ... The safest feature of the
shield wall is the worst feature of a shield wall ... what happens to
one happens to all ... the back is moving so we have to move ...
that or have them walk through us ... I shout an order to advance
... there's nothing I can do but go with it ... we right ourselves ...
the good land that is Scotland is solid again under our feet ... we
are through their front rank ... they pour off us like water ... we
are invincible ... and then, oh my God, somebody has slipped ...
ay, and at last the patience I have kept for twenty-three years
breaks ... oh Finn, how could you give this up? ... This for
Thorfinn ... that for Gruoch ... and this for what you would do to
us ... you grasping, ignorant illiterate bastards!

Sings

> Faces of greed, swords cruel and keen,
> There at Lumphanan surrounded the High King,
> Blithely the wall broke then ceaseless the swording,
> Spear unto spear spoke, bloody and blurred:
> Accept of our life's blood and we have rewarding.
> Screams high the battle bird,
> Reddened men's hands in blood.

and twelve hundred years are swept away.

> Humbled the homesteads
> Burning in Scotland.
> Red flame from smoking thatch
> Shoots high: for that day
> Dire danger failed not!
> Slain was the Ard Righ
> By the young lord.

No ... not quite the end ... but don't worry, not long now ...
they'll still be serving ... but there's a wee twist I think you
might enjoy ... oh yes, in a way I win ... my followers get my
body away ... and to Malcolm's annoyance it is taken to Iona ...
St. Colme's Inch ... the Isle of Kings ... and they give it a royal
burial ... ay, and he isn't even able to capture Scone, not before
my stepson Lulach has been elected Ard Righ ... The Englishman
is not King yet ... But it was a foolish resistance ... twenty-three
years of peace is not the best preparation for war ... within six
months every major stronghold is in Malcolm's hands.

Lulach is invited to a peace conference.
Of course he went.

Under Celtic law hospitality is a sacred trust, the shame of Glencoe is not that a few thieving caterans were sent prematurely to their maker, but the way in which they were sent.

But Malcolm has been brought up in England ... Yes, Lulach was dirked in his bed by the very man who should 'against his murderer shut the door, not bear the knife himself'.

Ah well, that's death, eh? ... but Lulach rests in Iona ... we're not far away from each other ... not that he's in any danger now ... because you see, Malcolm and his descendants are not here, are they?

Oh no ... they were refused burial here ... of course they were ... they are not true Ard Righ n'h'Alba ... Where's the Lia Fail? ... No, no, no, there's no place for people like that on Iona, they have to make do with plots in that fine new minster saint Margaret built on stolen ground.

Rest in peace ... if you can.

Remember what I said about disappoint a tradition and nothing is left but fear and superstition.

Holds up a copy of the play

Which is the true tradition?
This? ...

Pointing to himself

... or this?
Are you still afraid of me? Or will you have a stone now?
Bona dies et pax vobiscum.

Blackout and Bow

An
English Education

James I is sleeping and dead. There is a knocking offstage. He wakes.

James I: Tam ... Tam McBain, is that you?
I'm haverin ... McBain's deid ... I went tae his funeral ... Ay, that wis some night ... a royal night! ... If I remember ... and that's it, isn't it? ... There's something I maun remember.

    I'll forget who I am next ... Except that a king is never allowed the luxury of forgetting who he is ... A king is always at the end of a knocking ... There's aye somebody at the door, reminding you who you are.

    James Stewart, first o that name, son of Ian, son of Robert, son of Marjorie, daughter of Robert - the Bruce.

There is a knocking offstage.

Come in, come in. Yer King's no asleep.

He goes over to the door.

    They're beginning to take me literally ... well, owre some things. "Let the latch keep the door" ... That's what I said right enough ... God damn ye I was speaking metaphorically, I meant if awbody wis honest there'd be no need o locks ... I did not mean you to go round the palace removing all the bloody bolts ... I can imagine circumstances when it could be maist embarrassing not to have a bolt ... There are some things a king doesnae want to be interrupted at.

    Nae bolt, eh? ... another job half done ... very Scottish ... hell it's the New Year isn't it? ... awbody downs tools at the New Year ... well awbody but me, I'd have tae die tae get a holiday.

    Because I am your king ... I canna walk down the street but

you are after me wi problems, petitions and prophecies ... This very day, as I'm just steppin intae the boat tae come here, an auld woman stops us ... At least it's a prophecy ... well, petitions can be expensive, and wi the money the English say we owe them for my education, we should be grateful for aw the savings we can mak ... Ye dinna hae to do anything about prophecies, they either happen or they don't ... and usually we don't notice anyway ... well they're gey obscure ... prophecies wouldna be prophecies if they were in clear Scots.

I mean listen tae hers:

"Dinna cross the water son, or there will be a new king croonit in Scotland this New Year."

It was something like that. My Gælic's still no aw that guid.

"Huthart has telt me!"

Exactly! wha the hell is Huthart? ... Her auld cat?

Oh ay! A king maun tak tent o a carlin's cat.

If it was not a prophecy, I'd take it as a warning that somebody was planning to give me a New Year holiday ... but prophecies are never literal in their meaning ... prophecies are the progeny of your real rulers ... Oh no, I don't mean the Lords and Earls ... no, nor Hailikirk, though it uses them ... I mean fear and superstition ... the shackles of ignorance and prejudice that bind our country ... my real enemies ... what you call tradition.

One thing about being raised in England, you do not have people telling you what Robert the Bruce did all the time ... Robert the Bruce is dead ... James Stewart is your king and by God I'll drag this country into the fifteenth century and to hell wi all the privileges and traditions that keep us poor.

Of course there will be a new king crownit in Scotland, dear ... There is aye a new king crownit in Scotland at New Year, do ye no ken the custom?

I know it's a pagan one ... to hell with Hailikirk ... face o Christ it's New Year, no Easter and New Year is a pagan time, thank the Lord ... ay, no all that pagan. No killing, no sacrifice.

Just an exchange o gifts and a tassie or two o wine ... drink up damn you and be grateful ... I have given you peace ... I'm no at peace, but you can all sleep sound.

Whit a self indulgent flyting!

"I'm no at peace"

That's whit comes o being a king and a poet ... I canna resist a finely turned phrase.

Come on James, you're alone ... the truth ... and the truth is that I am beginning to feel safe at last ... I know, I know. I've been complaining o all the cares o kingship ... I may have been brought up in England but I'm a Scot ... and we Scots hae a great facility for complaint ... I have brought peace to Scotland ... a man can travel from Perth to Glasgow wioot fear he'll be robbed on the road ... ay, and your king can sleep in a room wi nae bolt on the door, as lang as he sleeps alane, eh?

Shall I tell you a funny thing? ... The last time I felt as safe as this I wis just a wee bit laddie secure in an English prison ... That's a paradox, eh?

James Stewart felt safe when he was a prisoner o the English.

Ay, but you see I was treated so very, very, well ... no expense spared ... and why not? After all it was my own money ... you wouldna expect the English to keep me gratis ... a prince's education is a costly business ... that is what has made it all so difficult ... but I was treated brawly. Scaith and skelp I could have tholed, but denial o liberty coupled wi care, kindness ... even deference to my royal person ... that is quite beyond the understanding o a wee boy wioot a mammy.

More knocking offstage.

Oh for God's sake come in. Who do you think you are that you wait to be invited three times? King Death himself? Come in ... come in ... come in.

And shut the bloody door after you ... I was brought up in England, remember ... I feel the cold.

They say that when a man is at the point o death his hail life will be played out for him like a Christmas mumming ... ay or a tavern reckoning ... I never ordered this ... I deny the charge ... Where is mine host?

Do you see him? ... there ... on that chair ... how can ye miss him? ... He's got a gold crown on his head, ay just like my father's.

"Whit dae ye mean stay here in England? ... I'm afraid I have to go to France for my schoolin ... they are expecting me ... I'm going to learn to be a king like you ... you are a king aren't you?

Do you ken my father?" I'm standin here babbling and he just smiles and sucks his teeth.

Ye know I play sometimes at not being a prince. I pretend sometimes that people are not heeding me.

This is not a play.

King Henry Bolingbroke does not play.

Suddenly he shoots out a gloved hand, one finger pointing straight at me. I think I am afraid ... no one has ever pointed at me ... I point at them.

"Why France? ... English education is the finest in the world" awbody laughs.

So they bloody should ... it is a very good joke ... a royal joke. My father died laughing at it.

And I am King o Scots:

Sheamus, MacIan, MacRobert, MacWalter ... High King O Scots ... Oh ay, no question ... proclaimed at Scone ... Electit by the Thrie Estates o the nation ... Unfortunately I am in England ... Where they have a King already ... mebbe even two.

Whaur's King Richard? ... Tell us that then?
I'm better off than him, eh?

Oh ay, I'm safe ... very safe ... see the door's locked wi a braw new iron bolt, so I can sleep sound in ma bed.

Of course I can ... It is the honour o Princes only to murder their ain folk ... I'm safe. King Henry and I am no related ... well if you go back that far mebbe, but we're no kin enough for murder ... the man I have to fear is my braw uncle, Robert Duke o Albany who is looking after Scotland for me.

No, that is not a young lad's fancy, no nor something my jailors, I mean hosts, have persuaded me to believe ... come on, ye aw ken Albany killed ma brither Davie ... Of course he did, mebbe no wi his own white hands, but he shut him up in a prison wi no food and drink, and men ... even princes, that are denied food and drink have an unco bad habit o deein. Of course I'm grateful for the guard at the door ... I trust you.

Christ I am so bloody naive ... I genuinely believe that this incarceration ... these silken fetters, are only a temporary inconvenience.

Of course I'm going to be ransomed.

The English have admitted that I am here, and as they have no right to detain me I am going home.

A week ... a month ... formalities you understand. "Considerable progress has been made, a truce is in the wind." Ay, its all wind, isn't it?

I thought there wis a truce already ... was our ship no taken in time o truce? ... and this has to be very carefully explained to me ... twice ... You see that yin would have expired by now so it doesn't count ... truces are fragile arrangements ... by God I'd better heed my masters. International politics is awfy complicated ... You see although there was a truce between England and Scotland I was on my way to France ... Do you get it? ... England did not have a truce wi France ... Awfy complicated ... Anyway I am not a prisoner, I am an honoured guest who canna go home till he's paid his reckoning ...

I must remember not to use the words like "release" and "ransom", our two countries are at peace ... well, we're no at war ... Just between truces, eh!

Ay, I have a lot to learn before I can be King.

Could I not learn it in Scotland?

"They ask an impossible sum ... ye maun understand your uncle Albany can barely make ends meet as it is ... we are not a rich country."

Poor laddie, I'm sure he's daein his best ... do I ken the complexities. I'm learning ... Just give me a moment ... ay, there are so many public servants to bribe, aren't there ... sorry I mean "reward", don't I? ... I wouldna want the Regency to toom his pokes ... Oh yes, I understand ... He cannot impose a tax ... Ay, they'd throw him out if he did, wouldn't they? ... Scotland expects her Kings, ay and her Regents too, tae pay for all accidents o government ... sic as the capture and imprisonment o young Kings in time o truce ... whit could be more accidental than that, eh? ... Oot o the royal kist ... Oh come on, Scotland's a very poor country ... much too poor to pay taxes, eh?

I'm not sure I want to go home.

For God's sake all countries are poor when they're ill governed.

Are you a man, or just Albany's dug? ... and don't look at me like that ... Exactly: just remember who I am. Yes, one day you might have to pay for that look ... My uncle cannot live for ever ... He's an old man and all this care he has so kindly taken upon his shoulders on my behalf has made him older ... Nae need to apologise ... I canna thole servility ... Christ man, it's your loyalty I want ... your heart!

Ay, my studies are progressing ... King Henry sends me good teachers ... I'll say this for the old bugger, he keeps his word: an English education is a fine thing ... my mind fair buzzes wi elevated crack. Did you know that men are wealth?

Commonwealth!

It's a braw notion, eh? ... Ay, mebbe you're right ... "Priest talk" ... Harry Plantagenet and my uncle Albany are certainly not priests.

Ay, very practical men.

Look at the bastards ... smiling at ilk ither across the four hundred mile divide between Stirling and Westminster.

You've pochled two crowns you theivin craws.

For God's sake, that's what you two have in common ... you are both conniving bastards.

Pardonnez Moi! I'm forgetting my expensive lesson again, aren't I?

Founders of new dynasties.

You are playing with me, aren't you? ... You weren't sent down here to arrange for my release ... you were sent down here to make bloody sure I wasn't released ... What's your price? ... an earldom?

It is a conspiracy of the middle aged and secure to thrapple the young.

A bloody successful one.

Get out of my sight ... Guard, get this man out of here.

I did not think English air could smell so fresh ... Are there any honest men in Scotland? ... Does no one remember my brother? ... He was murdered, mind, by Albany ... Have you forgotten me ... I am your King ... I have been for seven years ... A hell of a lot of Kings don't get to reign that long ... not when they have nice kind uncles to do their kinging for them.

(paces off the room) One, two, three, four, five, six ... seven.

King of twelve feet by fourteen ... and a garden with a high wall.

"Yes, your Grace, no your Grace" ... Ay, they're kind enough. But it is seven years since mother smoothed my pillow and whispered her comforting nonsense in my ear ... and that shows

I've been here too long ... in ma lug ... We aw need someone to notice us.

I never see King Henry ... my brother monarch chooses to ignore his guest ... mebbe if he did he might pity me ... It's one of the games, isn't it? ... Every month I ask to see him.

He's got to see me ... My education is complete ... I don't care if the man's deein, I can do him a wee favour, just tell him that ... of course I can ... Did you no say he was a guilt ridden old bastard ... All right, but that's what you meant ... roaming his castle talking to his crown ... you tell him James Stewart can ease his guilt ... This is one crime he can undo and be forgiven for.

Man, can ye not see it!

It will be summer when I ride over the border ... on a white horse - surely you can get us a white horse ... Tae Melrose, tae Edinburgh ... tae Scone!

> Scotland. Awake!
> Awake out of your sluggardy
> And tent the burdis melody,
> Whose sugart notis loud and clear
> Is now ane paradise to hear ... eh?

(Note: the poems written by James in the play are not as they survive in The Kingis Quair. I am attempting to establish a consistency between the rhythms of speech and verse and avoid a sense of quotation: those bothered by the divergence should presume the versions supplied in this text to be earlier drafts of the poems as they survive.)

A new age will dawn in Scotland, will it not? ... Ay, but there is a funeral first ... England will have to bury this mass of usurping corruption in lead and sculptured stone ... but then Scotland will be free ... Oh ay, among the old bugger's last givings out is a recommendation that I be sent home.

Then what am I still doing here?

It was his order.

A dead king's orders are so much wind.

I can go to Hell for my answer ... ay or Harry Plantagenet the Fifth.

What do you mean I am sent for?

I am not a prisoner to be ordered about, I am King of Scots ...

Right enough, what do words matter ... Liberty and a kingdom await me up river ... Let us observe the rituals ... I will attend him.

A clock strikes six

He keeps time anyway ... though I'll be late by the time I get to that table ... It's a good ploy this, I must mind it ... make a man come to you ... ay, and sit high so that he has to look up ... and this is a good touch, ignore the bastard ... Ay, don't acknowledge him, just make him stand underneath you, staring at your crutch while the clerks mumble.

What's that?

"Prisoner of war in the Royaume of England"

Correction, hardly of war, my ship was taken during a truce ...

Your father always said I was only here to get ma schooling.

Oh go on, what does it matter, we are not here to debate my capture, but are here to debate my release ... to the point ... how much do I owe ... It's money, isn't it? ... When it comes down tae it that's what politics is, isn't it? ... Money! ... and power.

"And whereas the Kings of England, predecessors and progenitors of the said Henry the Fifth, have been from ancient time, by right of sovereignty and direct dominion, Lords of the Royaume of Scotland, of the Scottis Kings and all their temporal possessions ... "

No way.

You dinna bind me and my successors to aith homage and liege service ... Yes, I know I can deny it when I am home, say I was forced, get a papal dispensation ... It would still be a precedent ...

Back to jail, eh? ... back to leaning on this window ledge, feeding the bonny burdis and writing wee tunes ... Did you not know I am becoming an accomplished poet ...

> The birdis, beastis, fishis in the sea,
> They live in freedom ilk ane in his kind,
> Yet I a man alane lack liberty.

No, that's just poetry, of course I've not given up hope ... Poetry's like politics, there are ways to put things ... Well you couldna just write get your skirt up ... No, you praise her eyes ... It's the same thing ... an act o blatant piracy (because that's what my seizure was) has become a favour to a brother monarch ... I am not imprisoned here ... I am protected ...

Ay, or forgotten about ... he's got other things on his mind ... His father pochled the crown, remember ... That is one hell of a precedent ... The crown is the well spring of order ... The Law ... If that can be thieved whit chance has an old woman with one cow?

He has got to prove that God, in his infinite wisdom, meant the crown to be stolen ... Yes he needs to do something very brave and distinguished so that people won't notice what a cold, arrogant little shite he is ... It's great to wave a flag ... make your own wind ... Everybody feels like a God when they make wind ... and when a whole country is making wind together there is a marvellous sense of communal power.

Ay, flag waving is wonderfully distracting ... The poor can be starving in the streets but if you can get them to make wind with you they'll not make wind on you.

He's making wind with all England behind him.

Follow, follow ... grapple your minds to sternage of this navy ... fair dotterin wi excitement, they are ... Ay, excitement, national lust ... It's certainly not patriotism, only a blasphemer ... or an English man would call it that.

Oh ay, this is that same sleekit sassenach greed and arrogance that us Scots ken all too well ... Oh come on, there's no real love of home or kin in it, it is certainly not ardour to defend what is near and dear. There's nothing to defend ... They're the ones doing the attacking, for God's sake.

He gets his victory.

It was a close run thing, on a muddy day when the battle season wasn't properly begun and the French were experimenting with new tactics ... but in the record books it is a victory.

So they hang out the flags in London town and get drunk to celebrate the battle of Agincourt ... while here in France we eat dogs, cats, horses, mice and rats ... a negg costs ninepence, a napple a shilling.

Oh ay, I'm here ... with a flag of my own, a sword at my side ... and two guards to see I don't use it.

"A rare opportunity to complete your education, your Grace."
Don't be naive.

"The Auld Alliance."

When England goes to war with France us Scots go to war with England ... At least half the boys on that hill are Scottish, lads frae Glasgow fair itching tae get at us.

I am here for the sole purpose of uttering a royal proclamation that they must lay down their arms and go home.

I thought he'd mair couth than this ... does he no ken what Scotsmen would do with sic a proclamation? ... Oh, they'd be grateful for it, bloody grateful ... we eat dogs, cats, horses, mice and rats ... remember ... paper is a very scarce commodity ... we'll no mind a few words on the back of it ... Ay, well just put 'em behind us.

Henry the Fifth does not like being laughed at.

No sense of humour.

There are about three paces between us ... King England and King Scots eyeball to eyeball ... counting each other's blackheads ... trouble is they took my sword off me at the door, and he's got a dagger in his hand ... Ay, and I've had a drink ... And when you've had a drink you see things different, don't you ... I'm eggin him on.

I dare ye!

Let's face it, the way my reign has gone up to now I'm hardly great history ...

This is my chance to get remembered ... murdered Kings are very romantic figures ... Ay, and it's his and all, let's face it he's a boring bastard with a silly haircut ... but Agincourt and a royal murder might even earn him a ballad or two ... Though they'd have to say we were quarrelling over a quine, and quines are not quite your line, are they?

"Careful son, this'll cost you at least two cathedrals."

That gets to him, he's even more touchy about his immortal soul than he is about that haircut ... You see it's Hailikirk that is paying for this campaign ... We are soldiers of Christ ... What's so surprising about that? ... Hailikirk loves war, as long as it's a righteous war of course, and what war isn't? ... Of course war isn't caused by greed and covetousness, what a ridiculous notion, you've obviously never been at one ... war is about comradeship, causes and saving souls ... well it is the way he does it, wi all this flag waving and the butcher's apron of war trimmed wi the spangles o chivalry ... He's in his element ... man's world ... no women ... Careful, twa cathedrals and a trip to Palestine.

And Henry controls himself ... Ay, we even have another drink together as if we really are comrades in arms ... Ay, pour away, I don't know where you get this stuff but it's bloody potent ... see's us owre another mouse ... and I try to tell him a complicated story about a friar and a jailor's daughter and he tries to laugh.

Ay, we get drunk together ... well I get drunk and he remains together ... I promise you that yin's not worth this headache ... because he still has it cried between the armies that James King of Scots has arrived in the English camp and requires all his loyal subjects to come over to him because they are making him very unhappy.

Of course they don't ... Why the hell should they? ... James Stewart! ... Who the hell's he when he's at home ... and that's it, isn't it? ... I've never been home ... They've never even seen me, never had a chance to wave their flags and make wind ... Scotsmen don't take Kings very seriously unless they've seen them and waved flags ... No, they obey his Regent, don't they? ... You cannot rule Scotland from London Town ... Christ it is difficult enough to rule Inverness from Stirling.

What am I smiling at?

I know it's raining, ay and we're out of cats, but things are beginning to get interesting ... You don't know the half of it, do you? ... when you read the chronicles going for a sodjer seems a very exciting life ... It is if you like eating strange beasties, sleeping in draughty tents and sharing your whore ... Most of the time's just waiting ... daily prayers are an event ... Ay, you fight once a month if you're lucky ... Well we fought ... yesterday ... It was a family affair ... no French involvement to complicate matters ... at a place called Baugé ... Of course you've never heard of it, you're not likely to either, not in this camp ... it was an English defeat ... a comprehensive stuffing.

See, why I am smiling.

Ay, they're not waving flags in London Town about this one. Here in the camp we're being told it was a strategic retreat.

"A brilliant rearguard action."

Och, awbody's too tired to argue ... what does it matter what they call it. They were sauté'd.

Oh I was there ... an observer ... and what I observed was Stirling Brig all over again:

The English lads are all fired up ... it was too easy ... They were three to one ... The thing was they have to cross a bridge to get at us ... Ay, they were picked off ... The ones that did get over peeled like prawns ... That's what those hooks on the back of pikes are for ... stripping armour. This is a good one for Hailikirk ... a lot of new widows ... I thought my good comrade Harry was going to greet when I put a sympathetic hand on his arm.

Stirling Brig, eh?

Ay, but like Stirling Brig, Baugé was not the end of the war.

He may be near greetin, but he still gets his men off in time, ay and in spite of his losses he manages to persuade the survivors that they haven't been beaten ... and that was a brilliant achievement ... that deserved more flags than Agincourt ... He may not be one of your inspirational leaders, you'll not find him in the forefront exhorting his men to make one more charge into the breach, but he's no a bad general I'll give him that ... I've a lot to learn from this one ... You see he's cold enough to run away, run to fight another day ... and a week later twenty one gey bedraggled countrymen are paraded before me.

All right, all right, don't get your scrotum in a twist ... it'll save men's lives I'll eat shit ... we're out of everything else anyway.

Give me the paper ... is this what he wants me to say?

Don't worry, I'll play his game:

"Down on your knees and ask forgiveness."

Of course I'm doing what he orders, for one I'm his prisoner, for another I've been well schooled ...

"Down on your knees, damn you."

Heroical gestures cost lives ... usually other people's ... but in this case yours ... "on your knees."

You promise not to tell anyone what I'm doing and I'll not klype on you lot ... come on, both sides get to write chronicles, you'll be heroes back in Scotland ... after all they ran from you at Baugé, just tell them that. They're too tired even to smile ... supine ... like a herd of cows after a bull has been at 'em.

Let's get on with it.

"You have borne arms against your lawful King."

There's a red headed lad, not quite as dopey as the rest ... He has very clear blue eyes, which I keep catching and losing the thread ... Damn those eyes, you might try and look a bit more penitent ... at least you are going home.

And I hand them over to the priests and go off and get drunk ... I'm not used to playing King ... I'm book learned for the job but the practicalities are different.

Two hours later I hear a great shout of laughter, and singing ... I'll say this for my guards, they're not bad lads, they did their best to stop me leaving the tent.

Two short uprights ... eight feet at the most ... well there's no need for them to be any higher, us Scots don't come very big ... Eight foot uprights with a long cross beam of new felled oak ... damp oak, its bending under the weight ... the weight of twenty gentle swaying Scottish corpses ... The weight of a King's safe conduct ... The twenty first is still kicking out against English Justice.

So much for a Royal promise.

This completes my English education.

I do not want to go home any more.

And you are wrong! its not shame or anything daft like that ... I have been schooled in kingship, I can handle shame ... It's not the King that doesn't want to go home ... It's the man ... I may be King of Scots, but apart from my French holiday I've spent most of my life in this room ... well, and that garden ... when I came here that tree was so high ... now I can climb it ... Ay, sit on that wall and take the sun.

Surely you can speir the only thing that'll keep a healthy lad from his home, especially a home he hasn't seen for eighteen years, a home he kens nothing about ... Do you know I learnt in France that my uncle had fought a great battle in the Highlands at some place called Harlaw ... I don't know where Harlaw is, let alone what they were fighting about .. I'm told I'll have trouble from the Highlands one day, but nobody tells me why ... My world is what I can see from this wall ... all my world.

Ay, I'm fair besotted ... that's what keeps me here ...
Worship, ye that loveris be, this May,
For of your bliss the kalends are begun.

This is ridiculous ... I've not spoken to the lady ... I'm shy ... my experience of women has been confined to jailors' daughters ... and poetry ... which I must say she has improved enormously.

She is the fairest lady I have ever seen ... and don't start trying to tell me I have not seen many ladies ... I am a poet remember, a very imaginative lad ... up here I have seen thousands ... so what's different?

She's got her claes on and she's clapping a dug ... isn't she gentle ... I've never imagined gentleness, but then she's a princess ... Oh yes, she is a cousin of the King, the Lady Joan Beaufort ... did you think she was a fellow prisoner? ... The Tower of London is a royal palace as well as a keep, people live here, not just die ... Let's be fair, this is a comfortable room, very peaceful ... and I have a very peaceful thought.

Oh yes the good monks who have tutored me would be very proud ... I am beginning to confuse my Kinging and my loving ... but I am a King ... and Kings do not marry ... they unite ... Oh yes, the union of the Thistle and the Rose might well produce a jag-free plant.

This is not fantasy.

I have my chance.

Dust to dust ... ashes to ashes.

Ay, it's national greet baith sides o the border ... no flag waving ... no wind because gey suddenly baith Harry V and Robert Albany have been summoned to their maker ... ay, or the deil, does it matter ... they're baith deid.

I'm enjoying this ... hugely ... for almost eighteen years I've been begging the bastards to send me home ... and for almost eighteen years they have been making charges and conditions.

"An English education is an awful expensive commodity"

It may have been, I'm sure all they tutors didn't come cheap, and except in France I've eaten well ... but they didn't need the money ... then ... no what they wanted was oaths and a peaceful border.

Let's face it ... it worked.

Albany didnae send those lads to Baugé ... they were Douglas chiels ... and I'll tell you something else, he didn't come scurrying down south to steal kye the minute King Harry left Southampton ... but you see the situation's changed: oppressing people costs a lot ... oppressed people are not good tax payers ... and the French are too stupid to appreciate the wonderful benefits of being governed from London.

Ay, England needs siller ... and I"m worth siller ... now.

Ay, time is running out.

Don't you see? The mair time you give Scotland to forget James Stewart, the less James Stewart will be worth ... Everything was nice as ninepence while Uncle Robert was alive ... Oh don't be daft, that yin wis far too canny tae seize the crown for himself ... He didn't need to ... He was enjoying all the privileges without any of the responsibility ... If people didn't like something he'd done ... he just told them he was doing it for me ... Oh yes it was always my name and my seal on anything that might prove unpopular ... Ay, a few people saw through him, not all Scots are fools ... He just bought the buggars off, didn't he? ... with my money, or royal lands ... Byzantine! The last man the recipients of such generosity would want to see installed in Stirling castle is myself ... I might just require some of my own again, eh? ... Now Albany was clever, you need to be a very early worm to avoid being eaten by that yin ... His son Murdoch is an eedjit ... give him another six months and there will be no royal treasure ... I tell you something else, his sons want to make him King ... Ay, maist loving ... they're good lads ... As soon as he's crowned they're going to kill him and inherit ... Well an inherited crown's all legal, isn't it? Harry the Fourth proved that one ... his bairns inherited, nae problem.

So if you just give me Princess Joan and a reduction on the school fees I'm aff home while I still have a home to go to.

And do you know it's as if my real imprisonment's just beginning ... It's a gey forbidding country ... Does no one build for comfort in these parts. God, even the cows wear armour ... What's wrong with me Joan, this is where I've wanted tae be my whole life, well the last eighteen years anyway ... it's as if some bastard keeps pissing on my grave ... Och, I'll feel better when I'm over the border ... Just that one hill between us and Tweed Water, what did you say it was called? ... who the hell was Flodden? ... a silly name ... Hey, but yon would make a braw spot for a battle, eh?

Och come on, let's no waste time stravaegin round through Berwick ... what's wrong with this wee ford here ... What do you cry it? ... Right, let's take Coldstream ford ... go on it will get me out of all the formal celebrations ... give me another few days as a private individual ... come on, I'm on my honeymoon.

Where the hell do crowds come from? ... I'm supposed to be at Berwick and here they are with their demands and petitions ... Well I suppose I'd better get used to it ... Wheesht! one at a time ... I've only twa lugs. You cheeky bastard ... whit dae ye mean "Is it true all Sudrons are born wi tails?" ... Whit dae ye expect me to do? ... Howk up Queen Joan's skirts tae expose your prejudice? ... Ay, and now the merely curious have been pushed aside for complaint.

Ay, my reign has begun!

"Wur fields are bare and wur trees cut down."

"No a brig on the Clyde a-body dare use."

"It needs twenty men in arms to tak a cart tae Perth."

Wheesht will you! ... wheesht! ... I'll answer your questions and right your wrongs ... That is why I have come home ... to right wrong!

And now I do a stupid thing ... I am too inexperienced to resist a gesture ...

"I swear to you, dog's life or no, the latch shall keep the door and the furze bush the cow."

Ay, I'm going to have to live with this one.

Still it gets a cheer and everybody loves me ... now.

Sae it is in ilka town frae Melrose tae Scone.

Benach de Ri Sheamus!

That means "Hail King James" or I think it does ... Anyway after all these years I have finally been crowned ... I don't feel any different ... and that's not true ... everything's different ... For a start Scottish servants talk back, they don't act like servants ... Ay, and you don't get cobwebs in the Tower ... This place is full of them ... Oh no, it's not dirt ... superstition!

"It would be gey chauncy, sae it would, ay, and unco ungrateful for the blood o Bruce to hae thir cobwebs swept."

But there is more than cobwebs need dichtin here ... The whole place needs a good Lammas tidy.

I call a Parliament .... Ane Sederunt o the Thrie Estates of Scotland ... Tae homologate some law ... You'd think after eighteen years of Robert Albany folk would be desperate to share in governance ... They're not ... no way ... The lords just sit and say nothing, hugging their great swords like so many effigies in a kirk ... As for Johnny Commonweal? ... Johnny Commonweal doesnae come, or he sends one man to represent ten ... You cannae blame him, not with his betters acting the way they are. You see it's not that any of them are actively resisting what I am trying to do ... Well not openly ... It's a wee game, isn't it? ... I slip things past them that English peers wouldna thole for a minute, and aw the time they are sitting there quietly reckoning up how many swords they can count on when they go home to raise rebellion.

Christ's cross! It's no that I'm trying to make this country more like England, I'm just trying to civilise you ... And that's one hell of a task for a man with nae money, nae army and nae friends ... I am not King of Scotland ... I do not own the land ... I am King of Scots ... protector of its people ... I have no power unless we are at war, in time of peace I am simply an arbitrator, who must be gey careful never to encroach upon the ancient prerogatives of earls ... and as none of these are written down my earls do just what they want ... Christ I almost wish it would come to a rebellion or a civil war ... There would be clear issues then.

This man enjoys the revenues of land I ken weil was my father's:

"What is your title?"

"Whit?"

"Your title ... your paper of conveyance ... your proof that it is yours!"

"Och, we dinna need titles in Scotland ... Ye say they have papers for every stick and stone in England ... och, the English must be awfy dishonest if they canny trust a man's word!"

Every time I think I am getting to grips with Scotland it retreats ahint a barricade of privilege and ancient custom.

I need money and I need my father's lands back ... No, not to buy new silk stockings for my English quine ... to put the country to rights ... Do you see in this chaummer the man who gave you these lands? ... Murdoch Albany. Stand forth!

You are accused of conveying royal land without right or title ... What say you?

Awbody is silent ... They are letting me get away with this, because they ken this is between me and Murdy ... a family matter ... His father killed my brother ... It's what they would do themselves, well they'd just stick a knife in him, but if I want tae play wi him they'll go along ... eighteen years deserves some interest.

Ay, we see things different, they think this is a refined cruelty ... I think it's law.

Murdoch mutters something about decisions of Regency ... "speak up man" ... and I have him ... "By what right were you Regent?"

You see my uncle had the authority of my father's will, an authority confirmed by the Thrie Estates o Scotland assemblit in solemn Parliament ... Ay, they were all scared tae mess wi him ... but he did things legal ... Did I not say? ... Murdoch is a fool ... He just took up what his father left.

"Your Regency was without title!"

But what this means is that every act of his government ... or misgovernment was an act of treason.

Do you speir the value of titles now?

I had tae do it.

I couldnae let Murdy live. Oh no, it wasnae vengeance.

Murdoch Albany brutalised my country ... he made himself a living symbol of the weakness of this crown ... If I had spared him I'd have been treated the way they aye treat kings here if they show their belly.

So they are calling me a tyrant.

Better to be a tyrant than a fool ... There is too much division in this country to have awbody's love ... a King that is loved by awbody when we're not fighting the Sudron would be slipping up on the job somewhere. If it was simply that the country was divided into oppressors and oppressed, mebbe I could have let things go on for a while ... but there's a third group ... ay, "the decent people" ... can ye no hear them?

"String them Up!" ... "Hack the balls off them!"

Listen to yourselves. You're aw becoming as hard, cruel and ... stupid as the man you want to punish.

Christ telt us to forgive our enemies ... Do you think he said it for the good of the oppressors? ... He said it to protect us all from the terrible temptation of private vengeance.

Look at your ain faces ... lips that hae forgotten the softness of a kiss ... eyes cold as a New Year's morn.

Ay, I'm sure because that's what's happening to me ... I'm becoming like my old comrade in arms, Harry the Fifth:

Oh God why did I ever come home?

I have written nothing this last year ... Och I sign things, ay and I started a great heroic epic of Scotland's struggles against Sudron greed ... Och stirring stuff if what stirs you is blood and death and slaughter ... nae love in it.

Don't you see if I dinna give men justice I deny them love. Whit if someone burns your house about your ears, murders your children ... ay, or rapes your wife ... is the crime no a thousand times worse if you do the same to them ... Theirs must do the same to you ... yours to them till there's no one left to kill.

I'm not saying murderers should run free ... for God's sake that's what Murdoch tried ... I am saying that in this imperfect world the law must take unto itself the responsibility of Justice ... and in Scotland I am the Law.

A woman comes tae me ... well a woman is carried tae me ... it's gey difficult tae walk when someone has nailed iron boots to your feet ... iron boots are a kind o drastic soutering.

Do you not feel shame that this can happen in a civilised country? ... Do you know why they did it? ... because she requested that two gentlemen who were bestowing the honour of their attention upon her daughter should cease their games.

Hunt their honours down ... I don't care if they are related to the virgin Mary, get them for me ... alive.

It takes three weeks ... they didna hae the shame tae run. Twa shivering men are brought before their King ... a soldier pushes them on to their knees ...

Can ye no see whit you've done? ... Ah, so you were in drink, I maun understand that the blood's hot when one's had a dram or two, eh? ... Are you sober, now? ... ay, and you're sorry ... whit dae ye mean, "mak reparation", do ye no ken the lassie's killed herself? ... Ay, she wis tae hae been married at Lammas.

By Christ you shall make reparation ... you shall make reparation to this crown.

Take them away ... Yes, the very best frae ma ain table ... They are going tae need their strength.

And I send for my Steward.

"Tam, ye mind they colts ye showed me, ay the twa greys ... I hear you, I ken fine they're no schooled for riding ... I wasnae thinkin o ridin them ... I want them in the tiltyard the morn ... Ay, noon."

The next morning I dress wi great care ... I put a mail shirt under my tunic ... and I make my way down to the courtyard ... Tam's had the foresight to have a platform erected for me ... It hadna occurred tae me there'd be sic a crowd.

God help Scotland, where's awbody come from? ... Och leave them be ... If they want tae make the King's Justice a show let's not disappoint them ... Are these monks drunk? Ay, mebbe they're in the right o it, I wish I was ... Whit's that yin doin? ... how can people eat at a time like this? ... That bastard must hae been workin all night preparing food tae sell tae this crowd ... no, let him be ... He's no worse than the rest o us.

The horses are led out.

Woah, hold that beastie, Tam ... stand back you fools, can you no see its temper ... back, I don't want anyone hurt.

Well, ye ken whit I mean.

Down on your knees and pray ... Ay, pray, pray for your King ... this is him ... Hard faced and stern ... and he has two men pulled apart ... as Scotland has been for too long.

You may not love your King but Christ's cross you are beginning to fear him, eh?

Ay, I ken now the power of this crown.

It's no in itself, is it? ... In itself it's just a wee circle of gold, of less weight than a fat earl's belt ... Its power lies in the power it denies to others ... to fat earls, gentlemen like our drunken souters, or dukes like Murdoch Albany.

I am not master of Scotland ... och no, don't you see I am protector of the Scots ... Yes, I protect people from Scotland.

I am trying tae protect you from yourselves ... Did you ever see me wrestle, eh? ... I'm a braw wrestler, no need tae let me win because I'm your king ... Ay, I'm a strong man ... I ken fine awbody needs someone tae hate. Ay, go on, hate me ... so long as you love each other.

Damn you can you no at least try.

Whit am I saying? ... Whit's got into me the night? ... this is Joan's chamber, a place o love ... It's New Year ... a time o hope.

We're going tae do so much this year ...

"Let God but grant me life and there shall not be a corner in Scotland where the key shall not keep the castle and the furze bush the cow, though I myself shall lead the life of a dog to bring it about."

Bow-wow, eh?

Ye maun forgi'e me, I cannae forget thon auld carlin yammerin in the Gælic ... I'm no doing sae bad am I? ... when I first came home I wouldnae have understood a word of that ...

"Dinna cross the water son, or there will be a new king croonit in Scotland!"

... and then she rebuked me for wearing a green gown:

"Green is the guid folk's colour, it disnae dae tae make the guid folk jealous."

Ay, only a fool or a Sassenach would despise the guid folk ... I'll hae tae tame them next ...

Come on, if they want tae live in my Scotland, they maun obey its laws like everybody else.

But it wis a fey meeting ... and it's left me in a black humour.

Knocking offstage

Tam, Tam McBain ... but you're deid.

And I remember, so am I.

A guid New Year to you McBain. You'll tak a drink frae yer King's cup?

They got me, eh?

Nae bolt on the door, but bars on the windows that I canna shift. Help me!

And one o Joan's lassies, that bonnie red-heidit bissom Kate Douglas, tryin to haud the door closed wi her arm through the hoops, a human bolt ... And me without a sword ... But I was aye a bonny wrestler, Tam ... I put up a braw fecht, did I no? I marked the bastards.

And michtily by the shoulder blades
His foes to his feet he flang.
Oh I smote them and trampled them under me
That a lang month hence they bare
A black their throats with the grip o my hands
Till the hangman's noose came there.

What am I saying? ... it's an ill makar that glories in blood ... Vengeance is mine saith the Lord ... Every man killed for this crown adds to its terrible weight.

Hey Tam! Do you ken what? I'm free ... James Stewart is free at last.

Fade to Black